To Daddy,

With lots of love

Diana

Christmas 1986

TIM BROOKE-TAYLOR'S
CRICKET BOX

TIM BROOKE-TAYLOR'S
CRICKET BOX

Illustrated by Borin Van Loon

Stanley Paul
London Melbourne Auckland Johannesburg

Copyright ©Tim Brooke-Taylor 1986

All rights reserved

First published in 1986 by Stanley Paul & Co. Ltd
Brookmount House, 62–65 Chandos Place, Covent Garden,
London WC2N 4NW

An imprint of Century Hutchinson Ltd

Century Hutchinson Publishing Group (Australia) Pty Ltd
16–22 Church Street, Hawthorn, Melbourne, Victoria 3122

Century Hutchinson Group (NZ) Ltd
32–34 View Road, PO Box 40–086, Glenfield, Auckland 10

Century Hutchinson Group (SA) Pty Ltd
PO Box 337, Bergvlei 2012, South Africa

Set in Ehrhardt, Garamond, Times, Bembo,
Baskerville, Helvetica & Sabon by
Input Typesetting Ltd, Durnsford Road, SW19 8DR

Printed and bound in Great Britain by Butler & Tanner Ltd,
Frome, Somerset

British Library Cataloguing in Publication Data
Brooke-Taylor, Tim
   Tim Brooke-Taylor's cricket box.
   1. Cricket——Anecdotes, facetiae, satire, etc.
   I. Title
   796.35′0207   GV919
   ISBN 0 09 163890 9

CONTENTS

The Official MCC Cricketers' Diary – Advertisement

Photograph Acknowledgements

The majority of the photographs which appear in this book were supplied by The Photo Source. Others were kindly provided by Harry Sowden, J. Searle, Roger Kemp and Fred Rumsey.

A number of celebrities are presently in Barbados with the Fred Rumsey touring party who are here for their seventh annual BWIA Pro-Am festival, which starts today. In photo are some of the celebrities as they pose at the Old Trees Hotel for our photographers.

From left are Godfrey Evans, Tim Brooke-Taylor, Nick Cook, Fred Rumsey, Bill Athey, Ian Gould and Trevor Bayley, all of whom, with the exception of Rumsey, have represented England's national cricket side.

Pakistan 674 for 6 as match draws

FAISALABA... — Monday
(Reuter) — F...
highest ever...
for six as the...
in the secono...
tably produc...

A monum...
Qasim Oma...
from Salee...
features of...
ended with...
the mate...
wickets.

The dr...
first ma...
brough...
St...

Test best of 113 in the 1983-84 series in Australia, while Saleem collected his ... Test hundred, his third at the ... second against India ...

... and their ... aheer ... ating ... ve the ... in five

... , to a Kirmani ... aleem to

Festival of cricket starts

The seventh annual BWIA Pro Am Cricket Festival gets under way at 12.30 p.m. today at three grounds.

The BCL, who have won the title on two occasions, will meet Davi... ford's XI

spearheading the Organising Committee, which also includes Alan Birkinshaw, Tony Cozier, Jillian Cozier, Richard Edwards and Coleen R...

Above: *A cutting from the eagle-eyed* Barbados Advocate, *30 October 1984*

Right: *Positive evidence kindly supplied by Roger Kemp*

INTRODUCTION

OBSCURE facts and figures are meat and drink to the true cricket lover, and as a bit of an expert in this field I always thought I knew everything there was to know.

With this reputation I have often been called upon to tell, for example, 'The True History of the Elephant Man And His Loathesome Left Arm (over the wicket)'. And just as many times I have held an audience spellbound with an account of the Yom Kippur Series of Cancelled Saturday Games. I know the Irish cricket joke. You may have read my paper – 'St Catherine – Saint or Opening Bat?'. I am aware, of course, of Denis Compton's Chinaman, and the equally libellous report of Ian Botham's delicious young Indian boy.

But I did not know I had ever played cricket for England.

The account, reproduced opposite, tells the story – the highlight of my life, and even I had forgotten! I did not, as I had so arrogantly thought, know everything. Since that time I have become a humbler, but no less ambitious man. I still want to know every single cricketing fact. I want Tim Brooke-Taylor's box of cricket, as it were, to be full to overflowing.

My first task was to discover the details of my own Test Match. This has proved more difficult than I thought for, apart from the eagle-eyed *Barbados Advocate*, it is clear that no other paper had a reporter on the spot. Perhaps there was a strike, a power failure or something funny in the water. That at least would explain my own amnesia. At the time of going to press the only extra positive evidence is a photograph discovered and kindly donated by a Mr Roger Kemp, showing me in an England sweater. He can provide no further information other than that the picture was taken over ten years ago.

However, during the last twelve months my time has not been wasted, for while searching in vain for proof positive of my own international cricket career, I have been rewarded with the discovery of many new and thrilling pieces of cricketing knowledge. Throughout the world I have very generously been given free access to journals, diaries, backs of envelopes and one particularly helpful, if rather unpleasant, chewing-gum wrapper.

The publisher of this book on hearing of these finds approached and persuaded me that it was my duty as a cricket lover to share the contents of my cricket box with everyone, regardless of race, creed or colour. I am grateful to him for bearing the costs of producing this catalogue of cricket goodies.

This book is not for those people who have no interest in cricket (international terrorists, rapists, estate agents, etc). But for everyone else I hope it will prove an invaluable addition to their cricket library.

TIM BROOKE-TAYLOR
'No Balls'
Trevor Bailey Close
Lower Rumsey
Berks
April 1986

CHAPTER ONE

MY TEN FAVOURITE AND MOST UNUSUAL CRICKET GROUNDS

THIS selection has been difficult and many, I am sure, will quarrel with my final choice. Some will argue that the Cairo Camels' lovely old ground with its pyramid square is an obvious contender – perhaps too obvious – and that is why I have chosen to exclude it. I also anticipate a large postbag querying my omission of the Philetus Oval. In my defence I think most would agree the ground itself was pretty ordinary. Certainly the discovery of the twenty-two skulls of 'The Cricket People' as Schliemann called them lends credence to the legendary Human Sacrifice Test. But recent carbon dating of Sir Arthur Evans's 'stump' shows it was made at least 500 years later and must have fallen from a higher level.

These that follow, then, are the ones I have selected to represent my choice of 'my ten favourite and unusual grounds'.

THE SWAMPS
Adelaide

Took its name from the marshy feature that was there beforehand, the swampy grass and thick weed making fielding exceptionally difficult even on fine days. After rain the situation became far worse, a smart drive necessitating a brisk swim by the outfielder (thus originating the new sport of 'water cricket' for a few brief years). The Swamps was abandoned in 1936 when the pitch became crocodile-infested on the pavilion side forcing fielding teams to place all fielders to leg, a situ-

ation which led to unnaturally high scores. The crocodiles became reasonably proficient fielders, and I found at least six examples of a catch having been called successfully for a ball lodged in the animal's gullet and recorded in the club record books.

An exciting match at The Swamps, Adelaide. The crocodile is fielding at square leg

THE RACECOURSE GROUND
Johannesburg

Built in 1903 by Vandern Van der Van der Post – a Boer farmer from the Svelte Velte. The ground was to be the best money might buy and boasted a diamond-encrusted kit room and the

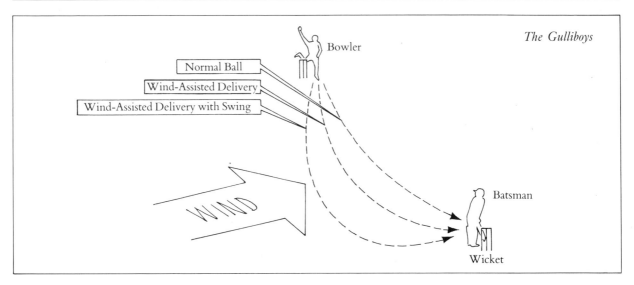

first gold-plated sightscreen, a glittering feature that contributed so much to many an early batsman's dismissal.

THE GULLIBOYS
Barbados

A graceful, well-proportioned ground, the only fault of which lies in the brisk on-shore breeze experienced in the late afternoon that can cruelly affect a bowler's figures. Local players have been able to accommodate the zephyr that by tradition blows across the square. Bowlers adapting themselves to the conditions bowl several yards into the wind, the ball then swinging suddenly back towards the stumps at the last possible moment. Tourists visiting the island and playing the crease have long commented on the unnerving experience which

has secured their complete collapse within five minutes of the onset of the on-shore gusts.

THE PUNGIJ'S HOLLOW
Bangalore

Built in 1896, it featured in many exciting Test series during colonial rule. Often called the most beautiful cricket ground in the world, it suffers from an extremely sharp fall at the scoreboard end rendering bowlers quite invisible to the facing batsman at least until the very last minute. Home teams have for long selected minute or dwarf bowlers for this very reason, their approach concealed till the last moment, at which point the batsman discovers the ball suddenly pitching towards him, delivered with feverish accuracy from an unusually low angle.

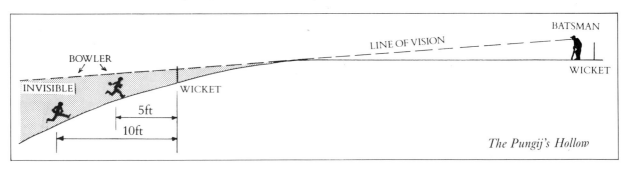

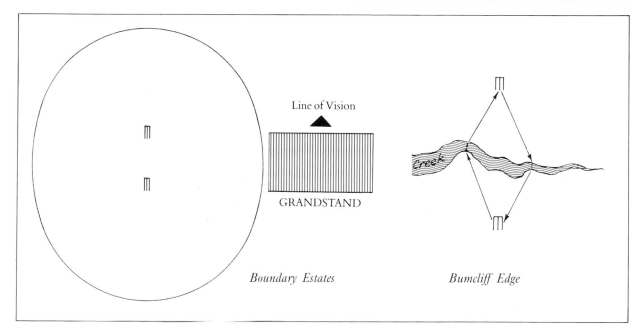

Line of Vision

GRANDSTAND

Boundary Estates

Bumcliff Edge

THE COWDRAYS
New Zealand

Players visiting the Cowdrays for the first time are often rendered speechless by the beauty of the rich setting, the ground set as it is amidst the gentle hillocks of the rolling Wellington countryside. It is fair to say they would revel far less were they to realise that over the years these same undulations have allowed local players to employ a quite ruthless system of precision fielding – the tops of the hillocks allowing home captains to place field positions as would a surveyor or planner. Home batsmen constructing their innings have also learnt to relate opposition fielders to the position of the hilltops thereby allowing inch-perfect shots to be made by using only the merest of glances at the surrounding topography.

BOUNDARY ESTATES
Pakistan

This ground would figure on any list of favourites were it not for the curiously built grandstand constructed at right angles to the wicket. The grandstand, quite remarkable in its splendour, was built at such an angle by error and was deemed too expensive to relocate. Nor could the pitch, hemmed in as it was, be repositioned. For many years, committee members have endured the discomfort of craning their necks to watch the cricket, the local 'cricket neck' regarded as something of a mark of social standing, indicating one's presence on the club committee. Indeed, the number of people to be found in the town feigning stiff necks simply to assume a false social standing is a tribute to the honour the affliction has gained: an unusually large number of street accidents being a further testimony to the 'neckers',' inability to look 'both ways'.

BUMCLIFF EDGE
Cromer, East Anglia

This long abandoned ground was almost lost to the club in 1956 when a tidal creek broke through the pitch during the course of a local league game, completely separating the ends of the wicket. For ten years the club persisted despite the inconvenience, batsmen having to make a risky 6-ft jump across the creek in their sprint between wickets. The near drowning of two batsmen in 1966, and the subsequent arrival of an inshore rescue helicopter on the pitch to pluck the two to safety (during which time a fierce squabble developed as to whether the two batsmen had in fact crossed) saw an end to the club and abandonment of the wicket. Each summer a memorial match is played on what is left of the wicket in recognition of the former club, rowing boats now providing a more dignified passage for both batsmen and bowlers.

THE BASSOCKS GROUND
Darwin, Australia

The pitch is used out-of-season as an auxiliary runway for the local Darwin airport, and many an early season match has been interrupted by the impromptu arrival of an aircraft on the wicket. Indeed, in one match in 1973 an exciting race took place when a local batsman achieved a new record of 0.00000012 seconds for his run between the wickets, while being pursued by an incoming Qantas cargo flight. Visiting teams are advised to consult the local secretary regarding the laws relating to air traffic before a game starts. In the past, a number of unhappy arguments have taken place with batsmen given run out when they have simply left the crease to dive for cover from low-flying aircraft.

THE MARKET PLACE
Ranjipoona

This was built in 1889 by a local builder who misheard the instructions and believed he was constructing a croquet pitch, thus accounting for the lack of any recognisable wicket and the unusually small boundary, which made high scoring a formality. No team took a wicket at the ground for the first forty-seven years, until the local chairman of the club, alarmed at the ridicule which his team attracted, decided to introduce a scaled-down set of bats, balls and stumps. The game proved immediately popular and the new 'mini' cricket – rather like playing marbles with toothpicks – was born.

The uniqueness of all these grounds highlights yet again the variety in our game of games. For the spectator, a lovely setting can make his day; but for the players it's the small strip in the middle, the wicket, that is all-important.

THE COUNTY WICKETS

Our American cousins are right to admire their baseball. It's a fine game, but hardly a thinking man's game, for the ball can only be propelled through the air. No baseball player, for example, has to worry his pretty little double header on a Thursday morning with the question 'But will the ball be turning by next Tuesday teatime?' My thanks to many of our leading players for their advice and help while compiling this list of county wickets.

DERBYSHIRE

Derby Slow, green and sticky, where ball will tickle slightly.

ESSEX

Chelmsford Fast and spongy, but green on sticky occasions.

GLAMORGAN

Cardiff Crumbling, usually green and spongy but turning sticky.

GLOUCESTERSHIRE

Bristol Extremely fiery except when crumbling. No sponge.

HAMPSHIRE

Southampton Less sticky but the sponge is definitely sporting. Tends to be helpful to ticklers.

Above left: *Middlesex – Lord's is considered to be one of the finest grounds in the country for rain*

Above right: *Somerset, Taunton – not the immaculate tickler it once was*

KENT

Canterbury Slow and easy with flat green pace. Tends to turn when the sponge gets ticklish.

LANCASHIRE

Manchester Can rapidly turn to sponge when the tickle is tricky.

LEICESTERSHIRE

Leicester Generally green and crumbling but can stick to the sponge when rolled.

MIDDLESEX

Lord's Always likely to turn into sponge. Very ticklish on the third day.

NORTHAMPTONSHIRE

Northampton Slow, sandy turner with plenty of fresh tickle.

NOTTINGHAMSHIRE

Trent Bridge Fast old tickler with plenty of turn for the average sponger.

SOMERSET

Taunton Not the immaculate tickler it once was. Very green behind the sponge.

SURREY

The Oval Immediately ticklish but likely to turn true in damp patches.

SUSSEX

Hove Once described as the ideal batsman's tickle. The bowlers' sponge has turned very green recently.

WARWICKSHIRE

Edgbaston A good bouncy turner. The sponge, formerly bouncy, has been re-tickled and is now very green.

WORCESTERSHIRE

Worcester Easy-paced piece of sandy turn, nearly always produces a Womble.

YORKSHIRE

Headingley In spongy weather can help ticklers' seams. The bounce can cause swing especially to stickies.

CAMBRIDGE UNIVERSITY

Fenners Slow, wet, sticky, with erratic green spongy tickle.

OXFORD UNIVERSITY

The Parks First-class tickler with plenty of Womble for the green tickler.

CHAPTER TWO

EXTRACTS FROM THE 'TEENY WEENY VERY VERY MUCH SHORTER OXFORD COMPANION TO CRICKET'

I AM grateful to the compiler of the *Oxford Companion to Cricket* for allowing me to quote from her shorter version of the best-selling twenty-three volume work. If *Wisden* is the cricketer's Bible, then surely this is our Prayer Book. The page numbers refer to the 1985 Just-In-Time-For-Christmas edition.

Ashes A generic name given to the Benson and Hedges and John Player Cup Competitions. (p. 3)

Backing Up A non-striking batsman who advances a stride or two down the pitch in anticipation of taking a quick run. (p. 27)

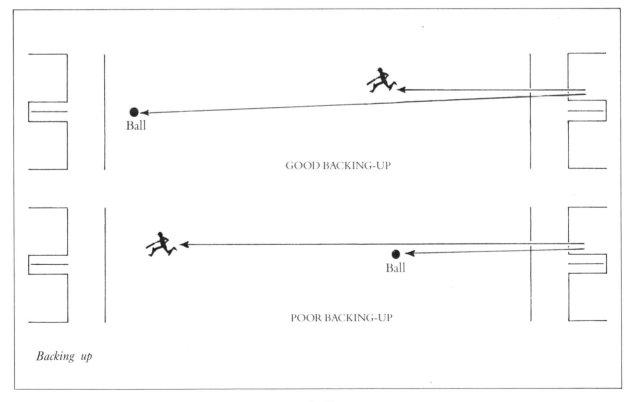

GOOD BACKING-UP

POOR BACKING-UP

Backing up

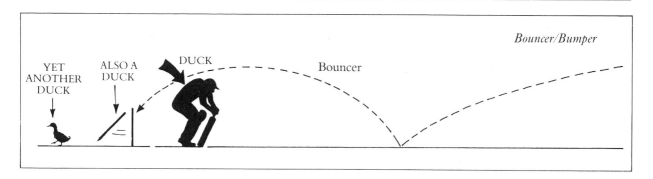

Bouncer/Bumper A fast, short-pitched ball that bounces or 'bumps' off the wicket leading to a 'duck'. (p. 31)

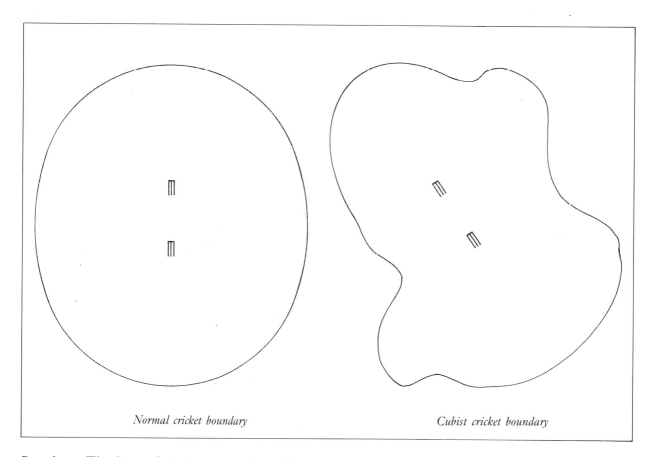

Normal cricket boundary

Cubist cricket boundary

Boundary The limit of playing area of a cricket ground. Marked by a white line, ropes, flags, fence, or row of small unruly boys. (p.34)

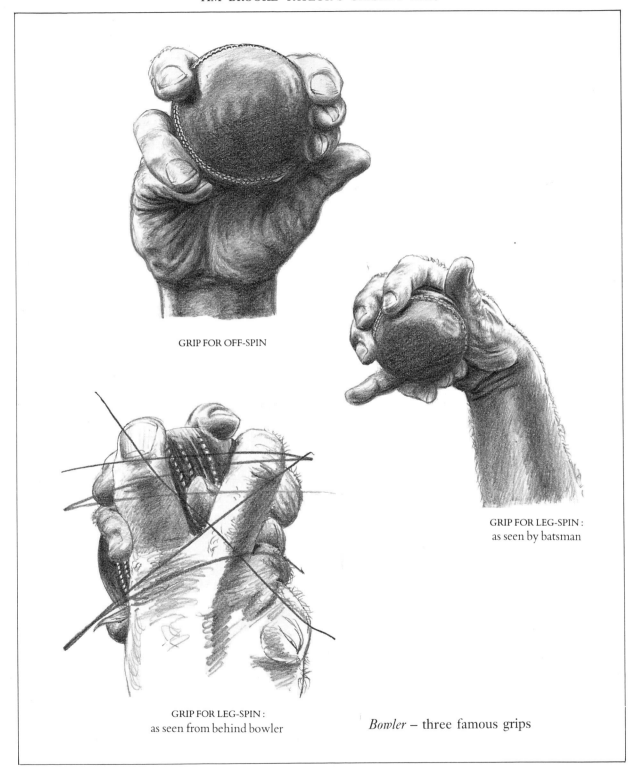

GRIP FOR OFF-SPIN

GRIP FOR LEG-SPIN :
as seen by batsman

GRIP FOR LEG-SPIN :
as seen from behind bowler

Bowler – three famous grips

Byes When a ball passes the striker without touching him or his bat, any runs the batsman can run count as extras, and are entered as 'byes'. Thus a batsman being out on a bye is deemed to have made a 'bad buy' or to have 'bought it'. (p. 37)

Covering A pitch may be covered till a match begins. It may not be covered during play when it might impede fair competition. (p. 42)

Play must not take place while the covers are still in position

Danger Area An umpire is required to protect the danger area from damage. In exceptional conditions the umpire may request players to play the entire game to the side of the danger area to avoid damage. (p. 44)

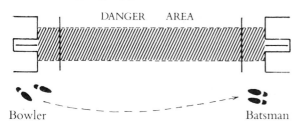

Declaration A captain may declare his side's innings closed regardless of the number of wickets down – at any time he wishes. Captains should avoid the use of the phrase 'I do declare' at other times (as in 'I do declare it's a nice day' or 'I do declare it's good to see you') as this has in the past led to umpires accepting declarations that were never intended. (p. 52)

Extras Runs made by a bowler. Runs scored by a bowler in this way are called extras. They do not contribute to the bowler's own batting score enabling him to top batting averages simply by his own mis-bowling. (p. 57)

Follow On Opposing captains may be invited to follow on their innings if they are more than the following number of runs behind after the first innings:

five-day match	200 runs
three-day match	150 runs
two-day match	100 runs
one-day match	75 runs

Not to be confused with 'fallow on' which is an expression that fielders use when the local farmer tries to bring his cattle on to the pitch in the middle of a game to feed on the fallow. Or 'fellow on' which is an expression used when trying to stop the 'fallow on' only to discover that the farmer has still managed to sneak on to the pitch. (p. 62)

Going Away A ball that leaves the bat. (*Going Back* – what happens when a batsman returns to the pavilion after edging a catch to slip on a ball that goes away.) (p. 67)

Guard Either (a) the position at which the batsman grounds his bat to defend his wicket; or (b) an object inserted into the jock-strap to provide protection. A batsman may ask for assistance from the umpire when locating (a), but not (b). (p. 74)

Hat Trick Trick performed by bowler (from Bowler-Hat Trick – to bowl a hat trick). (p. 81)

L b w (p. 83)

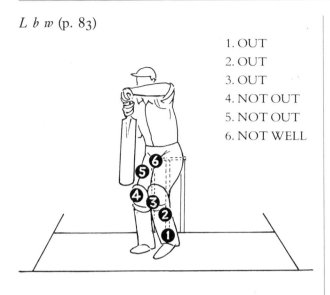

1. OUT
2. OUT
3. OUT
4. NOT OUT
5. NOT OUT
6. NOT WELL

Leg Cutter Person who goes around cutting the legs off opponents simply to upset them and cause them to lose balance (unusual). (p. 84)

Leg Trap Trap set to catch people who go around cutting the legs off opponents. (p. 87)

Matting Hemp strips laid where grass wickets cannot be. Often produces exciting climax to many games – the Matt Finish. (p. 91)

New Ball Usually more lively and therefore more effective for bowlers. May be taken after length of time specified by governing body. Players taking the new ball must return the old ball promptly. They cannot keep both and use them both alternately, or even worse, simultaneously. Old balls are often polished on the trouser leg to give them more shine and lift. Polishing with a duster, rag and wax polish is not allowed. (Except in ladies' cricket where regular dusting of all items of equipment is encouraged.) Umpires should learn to spot players entering the field of play in bright yellow trousers clearly made of lots of dusters sewn together with the express aim of polishing the ball as much as possible unless they are members of the Australian team playing night cricket! (p. 97)

No Ball What occurs when the old ball is polished too much and too rigorously. Also, an illegal delivery called by the umpire. More rarely called by a bowler upon reaching the bowling crease only to realise he isn't carrying the ball in his hand. (p. 101)

Over The number of balls dispatched by a bowler before he retires and switches to the other end. Early overs lasted four balls. Nowadays most countries have adopted six-ball overs. At the end of each over the umpire should call 'Over' (hence the fact that umpires wear white coats, or *overalls*). At the end of the match the umpire should call 'All over' (not 'Overall'), and remove the stumps (and not his coat or overall). The umpire should not call 'Over' in the middle of an over just to confuse everyone and have a jolly good laugh. (p. 107)

Overthrows Overs thrown away by bad batting or bowling. (p. 110)

Pair A batsman dismissed for a duck in each innings. (From the phrase used in French cricket *une au-pair* – literally 'a woman'.) (p. 113)

Runner A man running between wickets for a batsman unable to run for himself. Runners generally stay square from the wicket and away from the crease. They must not be current Olympic sprint champions nor must they wear athletes' singlets and running shoes. (p. 117)

Short Run A run where a batsman does not make a complete run. The run is disallowed where a short run is run. Long run – a run where a batsman needlessly runs for far longer than is necessary and continues to sprint beyond the crease and off into the distance. A long run counts for no extra runs. A long runner may often be pursued by men in white coats. These men can sometimes be the umpires. (p. 121)

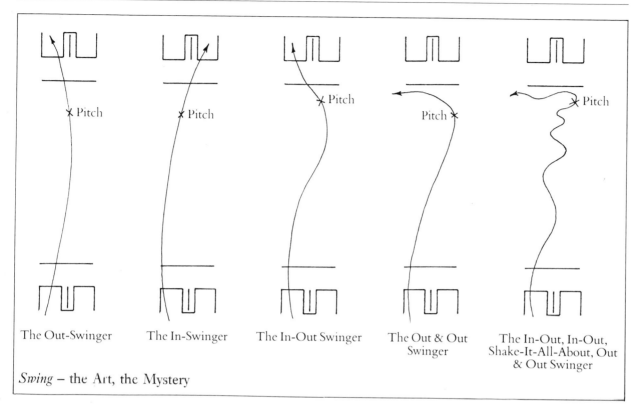

The Out-Swinger   The In-Swinger   The In-Out Swinger   The Out & Out Swinger   The In-Out, In-Out, Shake-It-All-About, Out & Out Swinger

Swing – the Art, the Mystery

Tail A name given to batsmen who aren't batsmen. (p. 129)

Test Match In international cricket, a match played between *at least* two teams, *but no more.* (p. 135)

Twelfth Man An extra/reserve, substituted if any player is injured. Often called the drinks waiter because of his job of carrying drinks out on to the field. (Which is one good reason why he is only twelfth man and not allowed to play because you can't have people slouching on to the pitch with a drink in their hand if they're playing cricket.) (p. 141)

Wisden The Cricketers' Almanac – first published in 1864 – and giving an annual record of the game.
    Also available: *The Pop-Up Wisden, The Wisden Work-Out Book, The Book of the Wisden Countryside, The Secret Diary of Adrian Wisden* 14½ *Not Out, The Country Diary of The Pop-Up Work-Out Edwardian Wisden Lady.* (p. 149)

THE GAME OF CRICKET AS SETTLED BY THE CRICKET CLUB AT THE 'PIG AND ANTELOPE' IN PALL MALL.

THE ORIGINAL RULES OF THE GAME.

The pitching of the first wicket is to be determined by the cast of a piece of money whereupon the first wicket is pitched and the popping crease cut which must be exactly 3 feet 10 inches from the wicket. The other wicket is to be pitched directly opposite the first wicket and at a distance of 22 yards and the other popping crease cut before it also. There are not to be any other marks on the pitch. Not even small ones. The stumps must be 22 inches long and the bail 6 inches. The stumps should not be inserted so forcibly that they cannot be removed except by digging a large hole with a shovel. The bail should be made of wood. It should not have 'Bail' written on it in big letters to help people recognize it. That would only make players smirk a lot and say rude things about other people not being able to tell what a bail looked like, ho ho ho, you know the sort of thing.

The ball must weigh between 5 and 6 ounces and be of a round shape. Where a ball is suspected of not being round it should be presented to the umpire for his opinion. If the umpire says that the ball is not round it should be withdrawn and replaced with another of correct design. It should not be handed to the groundsman to see if he can 'knock a few lumps off it'.

When the wickets are both pitched and all creases cut, the party that wins the toss-up may order which side it shall prefer to go in first. Where no coin is available the matter should be decided by peerage and that side with fewer titled players obliged to take the wicket first.

Laws for bowlers

The bowler must first deliver the ball with one foot behind the crease and even with the wicket. He shall always bowl in the direction of the opposing wicket and not away from it. When he has bowled one ball or more he shall bowl to the number four whereupon he should change wickets. If he shall deliver a ball with either foot over the bowling crease the umpire shall call 'No ball, Sir' and doff his hat.

Laws for the striker, or those that are in

If the wicket be bowled down it is out. If he strikes or treads down, or falls upon the wicket in striking it, it is also out, whereupon the umpire shall cry 'You are out, Sir, your pavilion awaits you.' A stroke or nip over or under his bat or upon his hands if the ball be held before she touches the ground though she be hugged to the body is also out. If the striker fails to remove his hat for any woman present he is to be given out. If he does not offer proper provision for the safety of any woman present while attempting a stroke he may be given out. If he is declared a pauper while at the wicket and cannot disprove the allegation then he is also to be given out. Neither tripping, kicking, nor jumping at a player shall be allowed. A player shall not intentionally handle the ball. A player shall not use his hands to hold or push an opponent. Charging is permissible but it must not be violent or dangerous. Tripping or attempting to throw an opponent over one's shoulders by use of the legs or by stooping in front of, or behind him, is however permissible.

Laws for wicket-keepers

The wicket-keeper shall stand at a reasonable distance behind the wicket, and shall not move till the ball is out of the bowler's hands, and shall not by any noise incommode the striker. In particular wicket-keepers must not evacuate any noise from their mouths or bodies or encourage any other to commit any such noise. Wicket-keepers are not allowed to remove or reposition any wickets during an innings. In particular they are not allowed to separate the three wickets and place them several feet apart to prevent the batsman from making a fair protection of them.

Laws for umpires

They are to be the sole judges of all outs and ins, and all ins and outs, of all fair and unfair play, of frivolous delays, and are discretionally to allow whatever time they think proper before the game recommences. They are not to use foul or unbecoming language or to make rough or abusive gestures at the other players. They are not to order any man out unless appealed to by one of the players.

They must not appeal themselves nor must they encourage players to appeal by hinting that if money is made available the appeal will be considered successful. They are not to blow raspberries in response to appeals they feel unworthy or incorrect. Each umpire is the sole judge of all nips and catches, ins and outs, wips and dogs, thargs and niks, diggos and poggles, and his determination shall be absolute; he shall not be changed for another umpire by bundling him into a fast carriage, driving him away from the ground and placing him on the fast packet to France, unless this be at his own request.

The umpire is not to keep wild or unattached animals on the pitch or to engage in the occupation of selling or trading whilst at the wicket. He cannot erect or maintain any structure that impedes the bowler or his action, nor can he become involved in the hiring and bridling of cabmen's horses. He is not to make use of a butcher, fishmonger or costermonger's services during this period and cannot entertain social guests at the wicket.

When both umpires shall call 'play' three times without a team entering the field it is at the peril of giving the game from those that refuse. The umpire may not erect a stone or wooden structure on the pitch with the express intention of making it his permanent place of residence after the game. He may not be a dead person (unless previously agreed to by both captains).

CHAPTER THREE

CRICKET THROUGH THE EYES
OF THE CAMERA

**AN APPEAL FOR LARGE WHITE BAGGIES
(LWB)**

The fielder appeals to the umpire after noticing the state of his own wicket-keeper's pants. The wicket-keeper indicates that the appeal is against himself by pointing at his own head. Although a batsman can be given out if the opponent's wicket-keeper has over-baggy pants, the appeal is rarely successful since the wicket-keeper's rump is seldom actually visible to the umpire at the time of bowling. To gain a successful appeal the wicket-keeper would have to turn his rear to the bowler during the actual delivery thereby exposing his buttocks to any tickle outside off-stump. *The law was revoked in 1978, thirty-four years after a successful appeal was made.*

TWO-STUMP   CRICKET

Mike Brearley looks on as Leicester's Dudleston successfully defends his two stumps. Two-stump cricket was introduced at the start of the 1976 season when the Test and County Cricket Board couldn't think of anything else to introduce. After eighteen games without a single wicket falling it was withdrawn.

1954 – AKMED ALI AKBAL

The Moslem Pakistani skipper gives thanks to Muhammad shortly after the Australian captain is given out lbw. This was the infamous 'wicket-kissing series' in which the Pakistani team were frequently warned about kissing the wicket. Indeed on the final day of the fourth Test the wicket was kissed so much that it became water-logged and the game had to be abandoned.

The Prime Minister's son Mark Thatcher catches himself out by mistake in a match against the Old Fallopians.

THE BISHOPS' CUP

The Bishop of Leeds, Peter Albright, drives a loose delivery from The Bishop of Durham in the Northern Bishops versus Southern Bishops match. The annual *Bishops' Cup* is played for each year by six teams of clerics; The Northern Bishops, The Southern Bishops, The Minor Bishops North, The Minor Bishops South, The Pope's XI and Geoffrey Boycott's XI. The match, appropriately enough, is played at Lord's.

MR BENDO

The incredible upside-down man (the only man to spend a full day in the field upside down, on his head, with his face turned to the wicket), makes an incredible 'blind' catch for Gloucestershire *v.* Yorks, 1951.

LONG DRAWS

The nineteenth Test at Chittapatta, 1908. Dogged by perfect batting wickets, the 1908 Indian series was to have been won by the first team to secure a victory. It eventually took thirty-seven matches for the tourists to score that win, returning home shadows of their former selves some two years after they had set out.

Glen Lover, perhaps the finest-ever cricket coach, demonstrating to a group of fine young cricketers his

ま训体る 手業とオ

Note the way Glen has paralysed the batsman by jabbing a finger into the nape of the neck, one of the most famous Shanghai cricketing positions. (see following pages).

West Indies and Pakistan. Often known as the 'exploding wicket-keeper's glove' final.

SHANGHAI CLICKET*

Few people realise that the true origin of the game of cricket lies not in England, but in the distant dynasties of China, where the ancient game of

幸世已知伏

(clicket) was played some 2000 years ago. It was this primitive game that travellers brought back to Europe and which emerged in England as the game of 'Royal Cricket' or simply 'cricket' as it was to become known. Few of those ancient Chinese rules now apply, apart from 泥并仰

表川保毛 and of course 平業と才

But it is worth remembering that 'Shanghai Cricket', as this ancient art is now known, is still enjoyed on the occasional paddy field. Among those positions whose name has at least been absorbed by our game, reference may be made to:

Goo Ga Li

A difficult, if effective, form of paralysis offered by the fielder who places his left index finger

against the batsman's rump moments before the ball is delivered. The result is normally instantaneous, the batsman rendered frozen with fear as he feels the strange finger slide effortlessly against his buttocks. By the time he has come to his senses and realised the cause of his embarrassment it is usually too late, the ball having cleanly removed the unprotected bails.

The Armpit

For centuries Chinese cricketers have known of the secret powers of Yo Ka Sha and Lhan Ka Sha, the two seas of total vulnerability located in the left and right armpits. By pressing lightly on these two points the victim may be left weakened or immobile. The trick is to discover the exact

---

*Taken from *The Art of Oriental Cricket* (Shanghai Edition), being a complete study of the ancient arts of

孔服保毛线朳狂犎世诤弞取洋
匡筒仔甫而丰新

(paralysis of one's opponent).

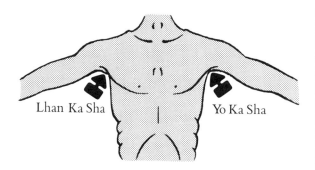

Lhan Ka Sha   Yo Ka Sha

location of the two seas and to learn how to place one's finger against each. Try with a friend. Explain what you are doing first to avoid any surprise or alarm. When he (or she) remains rigidly rooted to the spot then you can assume the power of Yo Ka Sha is with you. Do not practise on yourself. Apart from the difficulty of explaining if caught in the act, you also run the real risk of self-paralysis which can render you a prisoner in your own room for days. The name Yo Ka Sha has entered cricket language to mean a batsman who appears to suffer from just such an affliction.

Si Lhi Mhid Dhon

During delivery the nearest fielder makes a rush towards the batsman placing his forefinger firmly upon the batsman's nipple, or prone-zone. The batsman is instantly frozen in a position from which he is incapable of defending his pride, let alone his wicket.

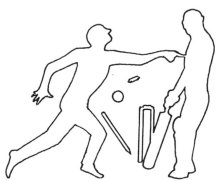

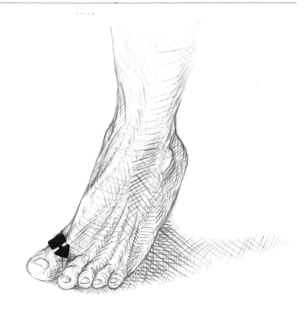

D'hjeffari-b'ho-Khott

A second ancient zone of weakness where a man may attack his opponent and render him immobile. The zone is found between the first and second toes on the left foot. Can only be effectively employed against barefooted batsmen, or those who regularly remove their shoes whilst at the crease.

La Dhis Thit This

No physical contact is required. Complete paralysis is achieved by the simple act of exposing on or near the cricket field at a crucial moment in the match.

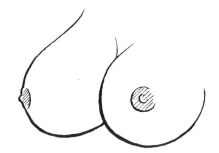

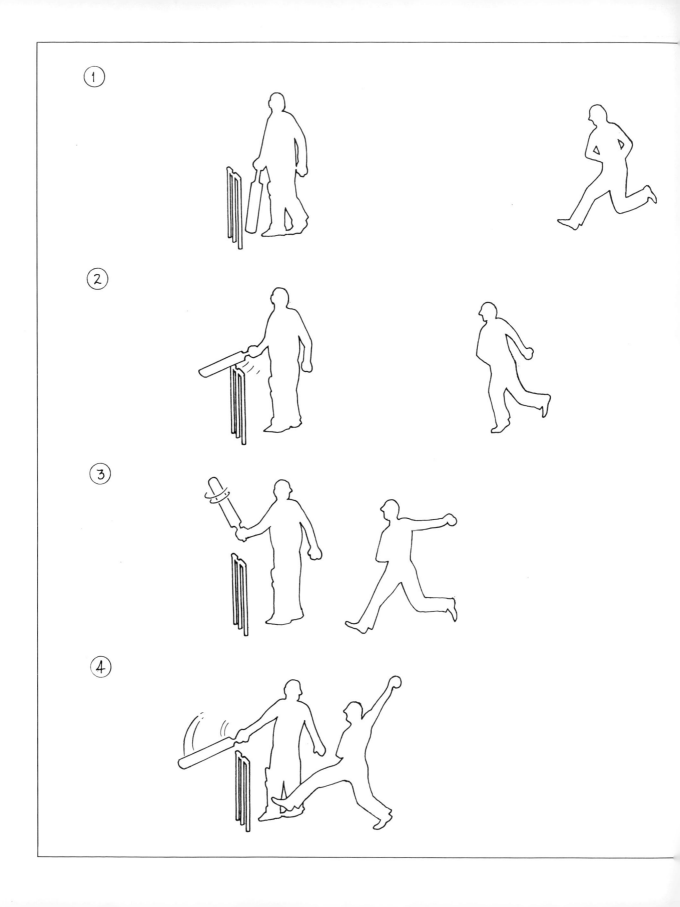

(5)

Slo Bo Lah

As the bowler approaches the wicket the non-facing batsman brings his bat sharply against the upper thighs of the bowler with stinging force. The result is similar to the paralysis of the earlier techniques but requires less art and more brute force. Likely to leave the bowler stricken for up to five minutes, during which time one should prepare one's excuses.

(6)

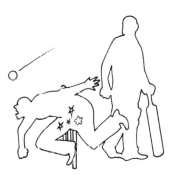

(7)

CHAPTER FOUR

THEY CHANGED MY LIFE!

Four articles that have sustained me in my cricket faith

M^Y articles of faith, I call them. Throughout life, every few overs or so, there comes a nagging doubt. Is there more to life than cricket? A nice cup of tea and a jolly good read of these pieces soon put things into perspective and one's off again on one's way round life's boundary. I hope they help you, too.

Bowling as a Fine Art

By R. J. Baggley (Lancs CCC Opening Scorer)

I don't think that any real judges of the game of cricket would deny that its several departments – batting, bowling, wicket-keeping, fielding – are each in themselves an art or a science, whichever you like to term them. They seem to me, every one of them, to require just as much expertise, in-born skill, polish, thought, care and exactness as do the sharpest handicrafts, the keenest brainwork or the most artistic occupation.

It is true that any lad or man can wield a bat; it is true that most men, having played our favourite game much in their youth, can manage against fair bowling to knock up a few runs. But my point is this: *how* will they make them?

I need scarcely point out to you the immense difference between watching a Hobbs, a Spencer, or a Knight batting, and watching any other well-known county batsmen who often makes fine scores. There is really all the difference in the world and even a tyro can see it!

In the one case you see a player making runs, it is true, but awkwardly, ungracefully, dubiously, or heavily. In the other you see the perfection of batting: you find the willow used as though it were a rapier; every stroke is polished in the extreme; the batsman is the acme of style and complete beauty when dealing with the bowling.

And bowling – one might fairly add – comes easily within the same category. It is, when rightly performed and whether or not successful in getting wickets, a lovely action, that of bowling a cricket ball – though I have not yet quite decided as to whether it really belongs to the domain of the arts or sciences! For undoubtedly it partakes of both. Now, it is just because I wish you lads to recognise this fact that I have agreed to write here for you a few notes on bowling, with what may afford useful hints and counsel. I want you to see that there is something in bowling even beyond the mere capture of wickets, though of course that must remain ever the paramount end and aim of the bowler.

Let us look at a few examples of artistic bowling and see what we can learn from them. I have thought more than once that I never watched an English bowler of his pace deliver a ball with more ease and beauty of action, taking into account also the wonderfully fine length he always achieved, than did the veteran R. P. Bramham. This greatest Leicestershire bowler of today belongs to the past – so far as regular first-class games are concerned. The more's the pity! For it was an education in itself for boys to observe closely R.P. doing his spells of bowling in big matches, his easy graceful run to the wicket, the stylish and charming way he raised his arm and sent off the ball, his fine poise – the very acme of an athlete – just as the ball left his hand. And the funny little habit of skipping one or two steps down the wicket on alternate feet, hands in pockets, eyes closed. Why, boys!

There you had bowling in its most artistic and polished manner.

As a really very fast bowler I used to admire greatly the way that Penhallion of Essex delivered the ball and took so many wickets. He would have taken far more of them, too, had Essex been as a team in that high class of fieldsmen which Yorkshire, Surrey, Cheshire and lately Hampshire have exemplified. But Penhallion was a real artist with the ball; he was faster than Barnham, but almost equally stylish, polished and attractive to watch. Whether you saw him successful or not in shifting the batsmen, you certainly could always rely on seeing a picture of artistry in bowling. His stylish half-run, half-walk, half-hop approach to the wicket, and his funny little unnerving habit of screaming through clenched teeth, combined with his tendency to mistake which hand the ball was in and deliver a handful of clean air in error, were a lesson in bowling few who watched him play were ever able to repay.

I remember that great all-rounder, the Hon. F.R.S.Q. Denby (now President of the Cambridgeshire WI) once saying that the reason why so many bowlers (and what a bowler he himself was, as well as a glorious batsman, and a very highly thought of seamstress) lost splendid opportunities to capture wickets was because they delivered the ball at the wrong moment. How often have you seen a young bowler let go of the ball one or two seconds before gaining maximum propulsion, or even let go of the ball while he was walking away from the wicket before starting his run-up? Too many to count, I should be confident to say! Denby laid down the maxim that there is an exact crucial second when the body is at its optimum poise, when every part will combine to make the delivery of the ball graceful, stylish,

and probably successful against the batsman. If the bowler catches that very second with his delivery, he will not only capture wickets but will become a real artist in bowling. If he misses it and delivers the ball while he is walking to his mark, or when he is walking to the pavilion at the luncheon interval, then he will injure his pride. And several spectators.

But, you may ask, can a slow bowler, a man specializing chiefly in breaks and spins and swerves, become an artist in the same way? Can *he* show up as polished and as graceful in style and attitude? Can his balls look as beautiful, and prove as successful in combination with polished action, as those of the fast or medium-fast bowler?

The question is not foolish on your part but if you have watched one or two celebrated bowlers of that type whom I shall now mention, you will undoubtedly acknowledge that the answer is in the affirmative. For what about Winkle or Poodle or Falstaff or Hinckley, or the late Alonzo Cooke of Middlesex? These names need no introduction.

Could you desire to see any slow bowler with more elegant action, more poise, more style, than Wilfred Rumbold? His one-two-three-four-seven-six-nine-two quick and easy steps to the wicket, as he delivers the ball directly at the batsman's head, are the perfection of an art in bowling. The way he raises his arm, the beautiful swing of his whole body at the moment of parting with the ball, the momentary pose of utter grace as it leaves his hand. And the startled howl of anguish as it smacks into the poor batsman's skull – why, you would probably never find them excelled in the whole range of slow bowling!

The very late Colin Bloodlust was equally effective in capturing wickets both for his county of Surrey, and

for his country, Iceland. His pupil and worthy successor, Frank Widecombe, has the same success, combining an accent of style and polish rare in a man with two pot legs.

You see, you must see, that I am quite right in arguing that bowling itself is in truth one of the finest arts. You, no doubt, have known several positions in various sports put forward as the acme of graceful artistry and effective poise: a fittingly dressed undergraduate skilfully wielding a punt pole on the Cam on an ideal day; a horseman, fearless and keen at the jump whose steed seems one with himself; a well-made swimmer taking a glorious dive; a nice pair of gentleman's buttocks thrusting tightly into a pair of elasticated underpants.

Those are all splendid sights. They are the acme of style and grace because the man (or woman if you must) is at one with the instrument or thing which accompanies him at that crucial moment.

Also so it is, or ought to be, with the bowler. The ball is *his* instrument and his pose with it at the moment of delivery might also be a 'sight for the gods'.

And what finer example to close with than that of the great off-spinner, T.J. Tremble, whose cunningly flighted deliveries have foxed batsmen for over a quarter of a century? Always of a grace and a poise quite unmatched, his sudden swaying runs to the wicket (glasses held firmly in pocket) crashing elegantly into the non-striking batsman and taking him tumbling forward in a cacophony of mayhem was a rare treasure to see. His studied elegance, even later in life when his eyesight had failed completely and he often bowled at the sightscreen by mistake, were the acme of true art to which bowlers should aspire.

GREAT OVERS THAT HAVE MADE HISTORY

By A.P. Hampton

The true cricketer has an eye not so much for the Titanic 'struggle' or the piling up of mammoth scores as for the possibilities that lie in the short over of six balls. The bowler is the real arbiter of cricket destiny; it is the sensational over that makes real history.

Years ago in a Test Match at Trent Bridge, England had been dismissed for a small score and Australia had nearly topped it for the loss of only one wicket, when Jackman went on to bowl. He clean-bowled Hill and Hillary, then had Nibble caught at the wicket, and Arjeeling caught at slip. Then he bowled Snipcock, Tweed and Hamson off the same delivery, before dismissing Curlen with the fifth ball and successfully appealing for a catch against Clarke who at that time hadn't even left the pavilion. Nine wickets off one over. It proved to be the turning point, and England won the match.

It was the same bowler who in 1906, had a hand in dismissing the Australians for the smallest score (three) they had ever made against a minor county. On that occasion Jackman bagged no less than eight batsmen off a single ball. It was Flintshire's only win of the season!

But the excitement of an over does not end with the taking of wickets. The lover of big hitting sometimes has his fill. At a memorable Test Match at the Pig Marshes in Bromwich, where England appeared to be almost beaten, Jessop came in and promptly hit Simpson round leg for four fours, off the first three balls of one over.

He even outdid that for Gloucestershire against Somerset some years ago when he hit one over from Cowley to the tune of forty-three – six sixes and a seven! While in a match at Scarborough in which that gigantic smiter C.P. Thornycroft played, all *six* deliveries were dispatched clean out of the ground and all of them into exactly the same gentleman's pocket as he waited for a number 17 bus.

In 1904 Yorkshire tried a new bowler called Sedgecliffe against Kent, who promptly took five Kent wickets for the loss of just two fingers. On seven occasions first-class cricketers have taken four wickets with four consecutive balls, but A.J. Wisley took six with just three balls in a match with the United States in 1887, and James Albright for England versus St Thomas Royal

Infirmary took no less than twenty-one wickets with successive balls when the hospital team were forced to follow on.

In a match between Essex and Cardiganshire a few seasons ago, Douglas, the Kent batsman, played a no-ball on to his wicket and had a second life when Rodgers missed catching him. He was then 'caught' off another no-ball and was missed at slip on the fourth ball. While on the fifth and sixth deliveries he was stumped and bowled consecutively, only for these to be given as no-balls as well. His amazing run of luck finally ran out in the next over when a meteorite fell from the sky and crushed him instantly to death.

During an over bowled by Taggard, the distinguished amateur, in 1908, J.N. Bignose thumped one ball so high that it was given lost and didn't land back on earth till three overs later, by which time a new ball had been employed.

But even the above was outdone in a recent club match, when owing to no-balls and wides sent down, no fewer than fifty-three balls had to be bowled to complete the over.

It is in some of the greatest of cricket contests that a single over has made history. Take, for instance, that match during Wedgewood's successful tour of India when Punjab were dismissed for only eight runs. This is how a portion of that game went. Partji caught off the third ball. Rest of the team caught off the next nine balls. The end.

Even more remarkable was the havoc wrought in the final over of a Test Match six years later when neither team scored a single run in the entire match and England just scraped through by a single leg bye on the final ball of the final day's play.

But for genuine excitement nothing could exceed the last over bowled in a match between Moor Hill and Incogniti six or seven years ago. Just one minute before the time fixed for drawing stumps, eight of the latter were out with the Moor men struggling desperately to bring off victory. The third ball of the final over accounted for the ninth wicket. The last batsman was in mufti, preparing to catch an early train, thinking it impossible that the game could be finished. But he rushed to the wicket dressed as he was, played the fourth ball of the over, then the fifth, then the sixth, then the seventh . . . then the eighth . . . and so on, until next morning . . . when an early visitor to the ground, seeing the game continuing, told both teams that the umpire had been seen leaving on the same early train the batsman had been intending to catch and that the game should have finished some twelve hours before. . . .

Sports For Boys
BEHIND THE STUMPS
HANDY HINTS

What makes a great stumper? Athletic reactions, a keen eye, solid concentration? I asked Willmott Evans, who has performed the task on countless occasions for England. He was quite sure what makes a great stumper: 'Position,' he said!

'Know your position and the rest will take care of itself', and he should know more than most what he's talking about. Make sure that your feet are correctly positioned. The best place is usually on the ground, the left one slightly to the left of the right one. A number of youngsters forget this simple but golden rule and end up standing on one leg. Others forget to put the left one to the left of the right one and cross their legs, or worse still, put one foot on top of the other.

You watch a first-class stumper and see how often he keeps both legs on the ground. And here Willmott has another tip for youngsters aspiring to the stumper's job: 'Move both your feet when walking or running'. Too many youngsters forget this handy piece of advice and just can't work out why they're not moving. Watch the professionals to see how it's done. Then practise at home.

Where should you stand? Well, most stumpers tend to stand at the opposite end to the bowler and Willmott agrees. 'It's no good starting at the bowler's end and trying to beat the ball down to the batsman's end. Start there in the first place.' And try and stand behind the wickets! Stand in front of the batsman and you'll deprive yourself of the chance of a catch or a 'stumping'. The best place is always somewhere behind the stumps.

Of course you can often decide the best place to stand simply by asking another player or someone in the crowd. But Willmott has another method: 'I usually stand approximately where both my feet are'.

And one final tip: always face the way the ball is coming. It's no good facing the opposite way then trying to turn round quickly and catch it the moment someone shouts out, 'Hoy, watch out you stupid so-and-so, it's going to hit you on the head!'

LBW: Leg Before Wicket

The origins of the term date back a considerable time to the formative years of the game. Early matches were invariably ruined by batsmen standing in front of the wicket and refusing to move clear when a delivery was made. They would offer no stroke and would simply allow the ball to bounce into them with resolute determination. Games of this nature could go on for several weeks or months, until the batsmen retired injured or the bowlers gave up in disgust.

Under pressure to do away with the habit which was rapidly killing the sport, and indeed rapidly killing the batsmen, the authorities made it illegal to offer one's body in defence of the wicket. Unfortunately this served only to hasten the subsequent and equally unsporting habit of placing a small infant, or more often a woman, in front of the wicket to act as defence, leaving the batsman free to thrash around to his heart's delight, or indeed he might even go away for a little while, confident that his wicket would still be intact upon his return.

This practice soon became widespread, giving rise to the expression 'maiden' – a term addressed to the act of placing a vulnerable woman in front of the wicket with a view to preventing a dismissal. Again, acting in the best interests of the game, the authorities stepped boldly in, several years later, to outlaw the practice of WBW – Woman Before Wicket, and shortly afterwards Infant Before Wicket – IBW. The practice of Foreign Person Before Wicket – FPBW – was not abandoned until much later.

A series of defence tactics were then employed to maintain the tradition of batsman impregnability – Head Before Wicket, Nose Before Wicket, Ear Lobe Before Wicket, and even Naughty Part Before Wicket (very unpopular), all of which were again challenged and withdrawn by the authorities. Leg Before Wicket, the final defiant gesture of this batting tradition, was the last to be made illegal and the term still exists today as a legacy of this most colourful period in the game.

(*from* 'Focus on Fact', 1953 *Playmore Cricket Annual*)

CHAPTER FIVE

I WAS MIKE BREARLEY'S GURU!

Few people realise that for many years when Mike Brearley was Captain of England he sought the help and guidance of a spiritualist, the Bhagwash Mahatma Bhatta, an Indian mystic living somewhere on the south coast. At several crucial points during his captaincy Brearley was to consult with the Bhagwash on matters relating to the game and seek his advice. I present herewith an interview with the Bhagwash from my recent copy of *The Spiritualist Cricketer* by the learned Sikh Is Ad Vice, together with three sample extracts of conversations that I was able to listen in on when sharing a phone extension with the Brearleys.

An interview with the Bhagwash Mahatma Bhatta

I remember many times Michael would be phoning me up to ask that I would advise him and I would be telling him how it is he should be doing to win. Sometimes it might be the position he is wishing of his fielders. Or sometimes it might be who it is to pick and who it is not to pick.

I remember many times I would be sitting on the stairs outside my room, the pay phone clasped to my ear, as I am explaining all the knowledge I am knowing. The first time we are speaking he is phoning up and Mrs Pritchard who is owning the house where I am living is knocking on my door and saying there is a Mr Brearley on the phone for you Mr Bhatta, are you going to come out and be speaking to him and I am saying to her, be patient Mrs P., I am practising the Praying Mantis position and my legs they are sticking together and I am not being able to move! And eventually I am managing to crawl out on my hands and I am saying yes please who are you being please, and he is saying this is Michael Brearley the English team captain, I am phoning about your advertisement in *The Times* offering spiritual guidance and advice on all cricketing matters, and I am saying, please to wait a minute I am getting the needles and the pins in one of my legs and I am not being able to move, and I am calling the Mrs Pritchard who is calling me all those funny names under the sun and is saying if it is happening once more I am being thrown out of her house. Then I am hearing the Brearley man asking if he should be calling back if I am having a great spiritual happening and I am saying I am not having a spiritual happening, I am having my legs rubbed with camphor oil to stop them being tickly by my landlady.

And at last I am able to speak properly and we are discussing all the cricketing things and he is asking me what my rates are and I am telling him it is five pounds for a field consultation and two pounds for a bowling change.

Five days after that first phone call Mike made a second call to the Bhagwash that I was able to overhear on our party line.

BREARLEY   Hello.
BHAGWASH   *Yes?*

BREARLEY   Is that the Bhagwash Ram Bhatta?
BHAGWASH   *No, he's moved and it's no good trying to trace him because he didn't leave an address and it's no good going to the police because that car was in working order when he sold it.*

BREARLEY   Oh.

BHAGWASH   *Who wants him anyway?*

BREARLEY   Mike Brearley.

BHAGWASH   *Michael, hello it is me.*

BREARLEY   I thought you said you weren't . . .

BHAGWASH   *No, no . . . that was a joke.*

BREARLEY   A joke?

BHAGWASH   *Yes, ha ha.*

BREARLEY   It didn't sound very funny to me. Look I haven't got much time – I need to know about tomorrow's game – when do we declare?

BHAGWASH   *Declare only when the declaration of your intent is exposed.*

BREARLEY   You what?

BHAGWASH   *Declare only when the declaration of your intent is exposed.*

BREARLEY   What does that mean?

BHAGWASH   *Do not seek understanding of those things you do not understand.*

BREARLEY   Look, do we declare before lunch, or is it worth batting on into the afternoon?

BHAGWASH   *Yes.*

BREARLEY   Yes, what?

BHAGWASH   *Yes, you do one, or the other.*

BREARLEY   But which?

BHAGWASH   *Beware the man who answers a question with a question.*

BREARLEY   What?

BHAGWASH   *Are you confused?*

BREARLEY   Yes.

BHAGWASH   *Good – confusion is the plant from which the seed of decision is sown.*

BREARLEY   You mean I should be confused?

BHAGWASH   *Yes. If you are not confused you wouldn't phone me seeking help, would you?*

BREARLEY   No.

BHAGWASH   *Good, then you are phoning me because you are wishing to be making a decision.*

BREARLEY   Yes, but what decision do I make?

BHAGWASH   *Well, imagine you were me, what would you say?*

BREARLEY   I don't know.

BHAGWASH   *Good – neither do I know what I would say – therefore this is meaning you and I am thinking the same way. The first sign of a man who is correct is agreement with his fellow men.*

BREARLEY   So I'm right?

BHAGWASH   *Yes – there you are see – you've got nothing to worry about!*

BREARLEY   Oh . . . good.

BHAGWASH   *The bill's in the post . . . goodnight!*

The next conversation I overheard was on the eve of an important test when Michael faced important selection decisions.

BREARLEY   Hello, is that the Bhagwash?

BHAGWASH   (HIGH-PITCHED VOICE) *Cor blimey cock, stone the crows, no. Why, who wants to know?*

BREARLEY   It's me – Mike Brearley.

BHAGWASH   *Michael, hello!*

BREARLEY   Wait a minute, who was that just then?

BHAGWASH   *Who was who just when?*

BREARLEY   That woman's voice?

BHAGWASH   *I never heard a woman's voice.*

BREARLEY   Look, Bhagwash, I need your advice. . . .

BHAGWASH   *A man who seeks but does not find is a man who truly finds himself.*

BREARLEY   Wait a minute, I haven't asked the question yet. . . .

BHAGWASH   *A question that is answered before it is asked is a question that doesn't truly exist.*

BREARLEY   What?

BHAGWASH   *Are you wishing to buy a video recorder from my friend? He gets them very cheap, no questions asked.*

BREARLEY   Look, Bhagwash, I want to know whether to put Botham in five or six. . . .

BHAGWASH   *What do you think?*

BREARLEY   I don't know – I'm asking you.

BHAGWASH   *And I'm asking you.*

[39]

BREARLEY	I asked you first.
BHAGWASH	*And I asked you the second.*
BREARLEY	And you're the Guru!
BHAGWASH	*All right, put him in both.*
BREARLEY	Five *and* six!
BHAGWASH	*Why not?*
BREARLEY	He can't bat five and six.
BHAGWASH	*The man who says can't is the man who does not believe in himself.*
BREARLEY	It's nothing to do with belief, I can't put the same player in to bat twice.
BHAGWASH	*All right, put him in five.*
BREARLEY	Why five?
BHAGWASH	*Why not?*
BREARLEY	Why not six?
BHAGWASH	*All right, put him in six.*
BREARLEY	But you said five.
BHAGWASH	*Wait a minute, heads for five, tails for six.*
BREARLEY	You want to decide it all with the toss of a coin?
BHAGWASH	*All our lives are like the chaff of the corn. We are blown so many ways, how many we know not and should the wind turn, then do we not change also?*
BREARLEY	So you reckon five?
BHAGWASH	*Or six. Whichever you fancy.*
BREARLEY	Right, I've got to dash, they're waiting.
BHAGWASH	*Hang about, are you sure you don't want the video?*

And finally this was the third and last time I was able to overhear Mike Brearley and the Guru talking.

BREARLEY	Hello, can I speak to the Bhagwash?
BHAGWASH	(CORNISH ACCENT) *He's just popped out to the shops.*
BREARLEY	Oh, when will he be back?
BHAGWASH	*Er . . . five years.*
BREARLEY	Five years!
BHAGWASH	*He's got a lot to get.*
BREARLEY	Look this is Mike Brearley – I want to speak to the Bhagwash, it's very important.
BHAGWASH	*Michael – hello, it's me!*
BREARLEY	Wait a minute, I thought you'd gone off to the shops.
BHAGWASH	*I'm back.*
BREARLEY	I was told you'd be five years.
BHAGWASH	*I took a short cut.*
BREARLEY	Look, I need to know about the field for the final day of the Test tomorrow.
BHAGWASH	*Two slips and a gully, silly mid-on, mid-off, cover, cover point, deep mid-wicket, and point.*
BREARLEY	But I haven't told you anything about the conditions.
BHAGWASH	*That's all right, I'm a Guru.*
BREARLEY	Wait a minute, did you just read that from a newspaper?
BHAGWASH	*No.*
BREARLEY	Then what's that I can hear rustling in the background?
BHAGWASH	*The man who wants to hear will hear many things.*
BREARLEY	All right, why go for that field then?
BHAGWASH	*Er . . . hold on I've lost my place.*
BREARLEY	You're reading it.
BHAGWASH	*No I'm not.*
BREARLEY	Yes you are, that's this morning's newspaper report you're reading.
BHAGWASH	*Life is full of coincidence, and the biggest coincidence is the coincidence of life itself.*
BREARLEY	Don't try and wriggle out of it.
BHAGWASH	*I'm not trying to wriggle out of it.*
BREARLEY	Yes you are.
BHAGWASH	*Listen, Michael, I'm a Guru I can say what I like.*
BREARLEY	Oh shut up.
BHAGWASH	*The man who tells another man to be quiet wishes only to be quiet himself . . . Michael . . . Michael? . . . Now where the hell did he go?*

After this the Bhagwash was never again to speak to the England captain.

CHAPTER SIX

SEEING IS BELIEVING

*An illustrated guide to some of the world's
most remarkable sides*

WHILE searching through the world's picture galleries for a photograph of myself in an England sweater, I was amazed to find so many photographs, as yet unpublished, of some of the greatest and most astonishing sides the world has ever known. Lack of space prevents me from reproducing as many as I would have liked, but here are a few of outstanding interest.

WEST INDIES
1934

The West Indian tourists take the field at the start of their very successful if somewhat limited tour of the West Indies in 1934. Part of the team's success was undoubtedly due to their use of twelve players in each match without anyone ever noticing.

HARROW SCHOOL
1957

The Harrow Schoolboy team take the field in the controversial match against Eton in 1957. Harrow were strongly criticised for setting up a number of school scholarships in which promising cricket-playing boys were allowed at school six or seven times longer than was normal practice. The captain of the Harrow boys on this day was a forty-nine-year-old 'first-year' day boy, while eight of the other boys were over fifty.

R.F. LEVINGTON'S XI *v.* REST OF THE WORLD
1953

Standing (*left to right*) R.F. Levington, B.F. Levington, C.F. Levington, K.P. Levington, F.A. Levington, F.O. Levington. Seated (*left to right*) Q.Y.X. Levington, C.N.D. Levington, N.B.G. Levington, S.O.D. Levington, C.O.D. Levington.

THE NOMADS
Winners of the 1912 Sir Cardew Bannister Trophy

(*Back row, left to right*) Atkinson, Pankthorpe, Stirrup, Arkthorpe, Bandubble, Bronkstop.
(*Middle row, left to right*) Pingbong, Yangnip, B'tangbingo, Niggawoop, Bobodiddlebonk.
(*Front row, left to right*) Niknappinoo, Grrrnarg-thargbucketbanana. [*Yangnip and Niknappinoo married the following year.*]

SIR LEONARD PIPCOCK'S XI
at Stroud, 1933

(*Left to right*) High, Honor, Hill, Livered, D'Alonli, Goat, Herd, Leigh, O'Daley, O'Daley, E. Hoo.

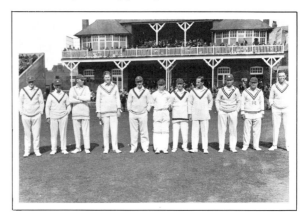

MINOR COUNTIES NORTH BY NORTH WEST (VARYING SLIGHTLY)
Winners of the World's Worst-Turned-Out Tournament, 1921

The team laundry basket was arrested by the police after this picture was taken and charged with causing a criminal nuisance.

DIPPY DIBCOCK'S MIDGET TOURING PARTY
1950

Selected purely on the basis of height, the team required twice the number of players of a normal team, each supporting a second on his shoulders to make a more suitable height. A cunning one-piece cricket outfit (not illustrated) was used to conceal this fact from the opponents. Here we see twenty players (divided by two to make ten) plus Dippy (in the jacket). A serious accident when eight extremely short players teamed up to make two full-size batsmen who then collided when crossing (thirteen broken legs, eleven broken arms, forty-three broken ribs, and seven cases of concussion) saw the trick rumbled. The team never played again afterwards.

G.F. LOUSTER'S WINTER TOURISTS
1929

Standing (*left to right*) Snipweed, Bonker, Shag-kettle, Plonkhampton, Grimfondle, Stumpknob, Bigstick, Thinwillie.
Seated (*left to right*) Bumfetlock, Snotgrass, Fartloudly, Stinkend, Grope-Constantly.
The team received the Arthur Bigpiddle Award for the least pleasant combination of names in a cricket team for five successive seasons. The photograph was taken at the moment of Grope-Constantly's arrest on a minor sex charge.

CHAPTER SEVEN

THE ART OF CRICKET AS ART

CRICKET has been an inspiration to all great artists. The six-figure sum paid recently at Sotheby's for Canaletto's *Caught Behind* comes as no surprise after the Getty Museum's record-breaking bid for Constable's *Haywain from the Bowler's End*. Even a small preliminary sketch in the author's own collection by Stanley Spencer for his unfinished mural *Christ Behind The Stumps in Cookham High Street* has been valued at something a little more than the on-the-road price for a 1935 Lagonda. I am particularly grateful therefore to the private collectors who have allowed this small sample of cricketing art to be reproduced for the very first time.

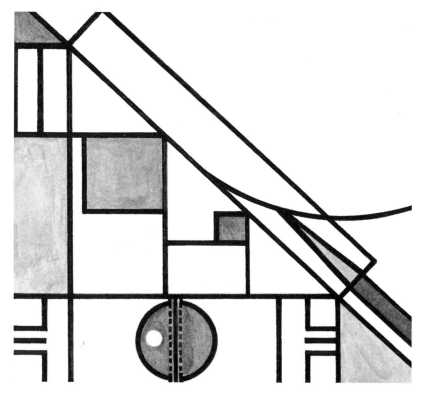

261 all out (Smedley 97, Croft 37 for 4)
Jacob Polcani 1952
(Institute of Abstract Art, Helsinki)

Corinthian Style of Cricket Architecture

*The Venus de Milo from the
Gasworks End*

The Palette of Headingley
1st Dynasty, c. 3200 BC

Bushman cave painting of elands
(playing cricket)

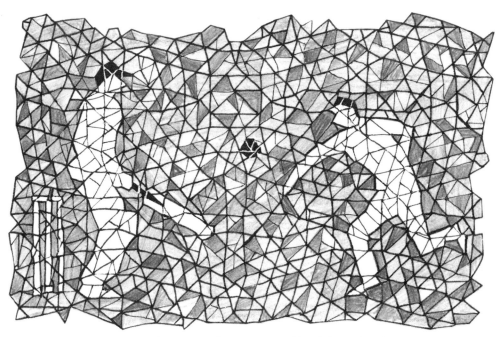

Romano-British mosaic pavement with a left-arm bowler at
Villa Verulamium, St Albans

The Persistence of Cricket
Salvador Dali, 1931

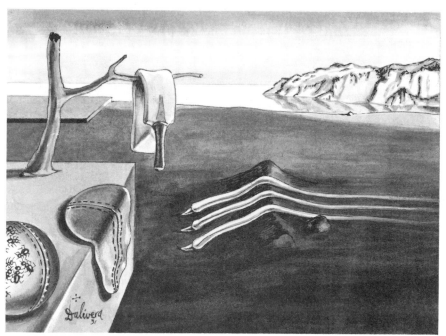

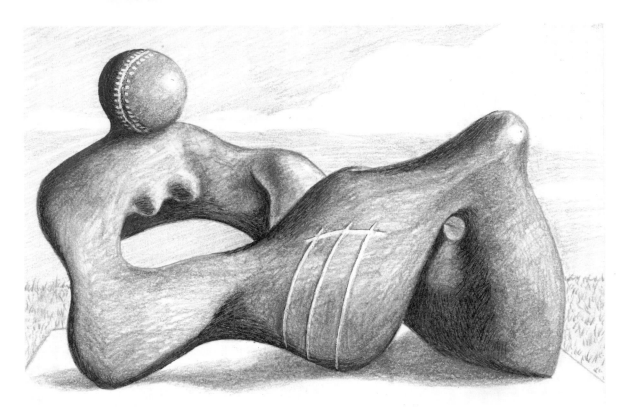

*Mother and
Cricket Ball*
Henry Moore

Pile of Cans
(Reproduced by kind permission
of the Tate Gallery)

*Toulouse Lautrec
cricket
scoreboard*
(Victoria and
Albert Museum)

CHAPTER EIGHT

THE ARNOLD TURNER COLLECTION OF QUITE OUTSTANDING CRICKETERS AND THEIR UNIQUE ACHIEVEMENTS

CASABLANCA is not the obvious place to find a complete set of Arnold Turners. Although I, like many, had heard the rumours that one set remained, snatched from the flames by Turner's widow at the very last moment of his cremation, there has never been any hint of their whereabouts. A Moroccan beggar assured me of their authenticity and his heavy club with its metal spike provided me with all the extra proof I required. The Turners have led me to accounts, spread world-wide, of some of the greatest feats of batsmanship of all time, many of which would otherwise have been long forgotten.

BEN SHELDON
(1923–)

Ben Sheldon's quite outstanding innings came during a vital County Championship Match between Gloucestershire and Sussex. Sussex needed a win to have any chance of taking the Championship, while Gloucestershire had already batted and set Sussex a stiff task. Sheldon, the last Sussex man to come to the crease, knew he needed to score 138 for victory, and had only three balls left in which to do it.

Opinion differs as to how he was able to achieve his quite outstanding feat of scoring those 138 runs, with two balls to spare.

Certainly the Gloucestershire field positions afforded him few opportunities for runs, and yet

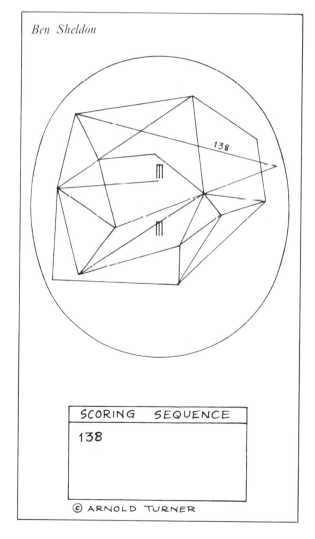

Ben Sheldon

138

SCORING SEQUENCE

138

© ARNOLD TURNER

when he drove tamely to cover off that first ball, he set in motion a chain reaction that allowed him to jog the required runs comfortably without the ball ever returning to the crease. For as the runs accumulated the Gloucestershire fielders simply threw the ball from one to another seemingly unconcerned that they should run either batsman out. Indeed, as the target for victory approached, the fielders elected to take the ball to each other by hand rather than even throw it.

An enquiry was held after the match as to why Gloucestershire had delayed throwing the ball back to the wickets for so long but the possible bribery suggested by many could never be proved. Sheldon later went on to make a number of large betting coups under similar mysterious circumstances and was last known to be living in the South of France with a former head of the Metropolitan Police.

ROGER REEVES
(1897–1964)

Reeves never enjoyed the same success with his country as he did at county level where, though useless as batsman and bowler, he was well worth his place for his prodigious fielding alone. Aided by a safe pair of hands and quite legendary speed, he was consistently able to make catches no other man would have attempted – his darting runs would take him fifty or a hundred yards or more in a space of seconds. In the 1904 season he made no less than 180 catches and in one game dismissed no less than nine batsmen. Batsmen soon learnt to play safely with Reeves in the field and for a brief period the 'Reeves Beater' became a popular stroke, the bat being held about waist high and the ball struck vertically down into the ground with great speed, the only problem occurring as the viciously pasted ball bounced back up off the crease and into the batsman's own face. In one season no less than fifty-eight batsmen retired injured in matches in which Reeves was involved.

Reeves was a quiet and gentle man off the field given to great acts of courage and bravery. He was married with two daughters and rumours about his legendary speed persisted even at home where he encouraged his young daughters to drop a feather from head height at which point he would run out of the house, down the garden and back again, snatching the feather before it fell to earth. He even encouraged his wife to drop valuable cut glass from the upstairs window while he raced downstairs and out into the garden to catch it.

After his success in the twenties, batsmen became more used to playing the 'human flypaper' as he liked to call himself and a frantic dash from silly mid-on to try and pick up a loose edge at first slip, three, even four times an over, was beginning to take its toll. Before the end of the decade he was a spent force.

In 1931, his last season in first-class cricket, he committed the almost unbelievable act and put down a simple catch. After that he was never quite the same and went to work in an off-licence, a sad and broken man.

GUTSFORD LONG
(1805–1839)

Gutsford Long's great innings occurred in 1838, the day before the length of the standard cricket wicket was established at 22 yards. Before that day wickets could vary in length from a few yards to a good hundred feet or more.

On the day in question the wicket measured no less than 188 feet, nearly three times the now customary length, with both sets of stumps almost upon the boundary. The effect on the bowling was disastrous, and Gutsford, realising this, set about it in quite remarkable fashion, standing mid-way between both wickets and hitting out wildly at anything that came his way. From his position centre wicket he soon accumulated a fine sixty-four that secured his team, the Old Ecumenicals, a distinguished victory against the Pig and Firkin Club, in a game of keen local interest.

The chance of a quick single was remote, yet Gutsford more than once risked a punishing sixty-

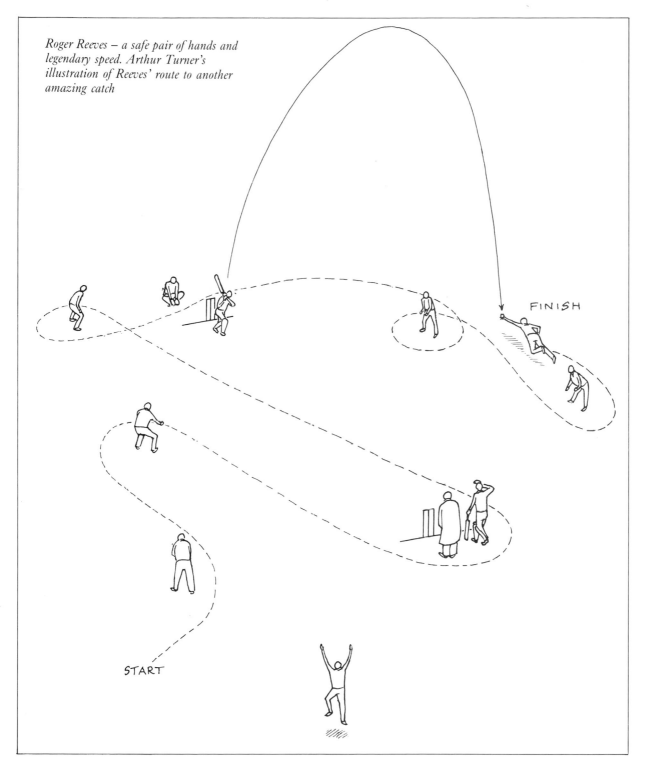

Roger Reeves – a safe pair of hands and legendary speed. Arthur Turner's illustration of Reeves' route to another amazing catch

FINISH

START

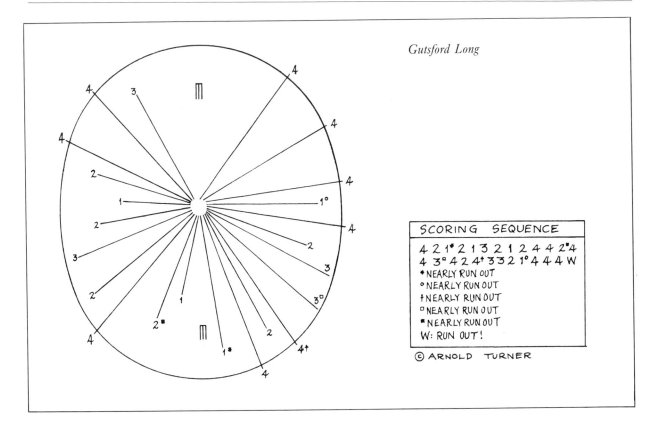

Gutsford Long

SCORING SEQUENCE

4 2 1* 2 1 3 2 1 2 4 4 2⁼4
4 3° 4 2 4† 3 3 2 1° 4 4 4 W
* NEARLY RUN OUT
° NEARLY RUN OUT
† NEARLY RUN OUT
□ NEARLY RUN OUT
■ NEARLY RUN OUT
W: RUN OUT !

© ARNOLD TURNER

yard dash in search of the winning run. Indeed, it was on one such run that he was eventually dismissed, pulling up short with wind. After the match, stumps were drawn for the last time on the 'long' wicket, thus preventing any repeat of Gutsford's unusual achievement.

HAROLD EMPSEY
(1823–1942)

After Gutsford's innings it seemed that little would be able to compete with his skill and endeavour in rising to such a unique situation. However, in 1863 the Yorkshire batsman Empsey carved a quite unforgettable niche for himself in the match between Yorkshire and a visiting Commonwealth side. Stumps had been set by two separate umpires, one selected by the home side and one selected by the visiting tourists. (*They had*

been unable to come to an amicable agreement on a suitable position for the eventual wicket and so it was agreed that each should be allowed to position one set apiece.) The result was unfortunate in the extreme, the crease at one end being some ten yards out of true with the crease at the other. But with both sides intent on establishing their rights, it was not possible to resolve the dispute, with the unfortunate upshot that at the start of play the teams were forced to accept a wicket with stumps ten yards out of true. Unable to reach agreement, they nevertheless decided to continue the match, for which a large crowd had gathered, as best they could.

The unusual wicket was beyond all of the Yorkshire batsmen, who found it impossible to make contact with a ball delivered at quite erratic length and pitch by the naturally confused bowlers. All, that is, except Empsey, who quickly sized up the situation, and taking not the traditional stationary

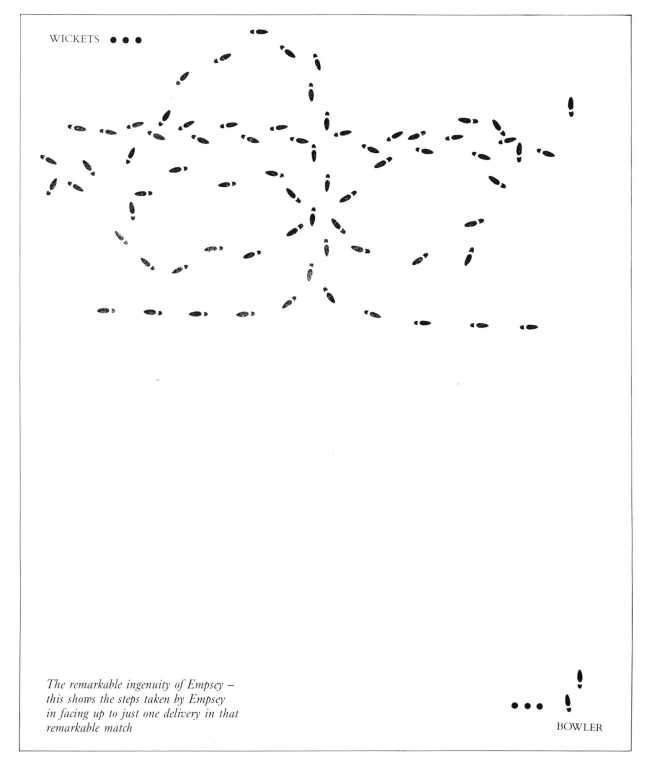

WICKETS ● ● ●

The remarkable ingenuity of Empsey –
this shows the steps taken by Empsey
in facing up to just one delivery in that
remarkable match

BOWLER

guard but running up and down between creases, attempted to hit the ball baseball style and accumulated a quite remarkable total of forty-five before eventually falling to the quick wit of the opposing wicket-keeper who stumped him as he ran about in a state of over-excitement.

The visitors asked to bat on such a wicket showed little resolve or determination and were roundly dismissed in a state of great confusion for the sum of just twelve runs (all byes). Empsey's feat in quickly adapting to a unique situation makes his innings remarkable less for the quantity of runs scored than for the agility of a batsman to adapt to an unusual situation. For years afterwards Empsey's batting never quite recovered from the strain of the match and for two seasons he continued to run up and down the crease swinging his bat at waist height in a display of great bravado that more often than not ended in a duck.

Right: *The colourful Harold Empsey*

SCORING SEQUENCE
1012003 0012003 00
1200131 002 000 000
0001000 2000 123
0001000 2020 3 32
0010001 00000 W
W: STUMPED WHILE RUNNING UP & DOWN WICKET VERY CONFUSED

© ARNOLD TURNER

Harold Empsey

ALEX SHAWCROFT
(*1897–1933*)
(Australia)

Alex's remarkable innings owed less to a versatility of style and more to an ingenuity of engineering. By carving a series of rivulet edges upon his bat, and by employing a crude slicing stroke not dissimilar to that used in the propulsion of the common boomerang, he was able to execute a range of startling shots that confused the opposing fielders and delighted his own supporters.

Playing across the line with what was to become known as his 'rubber bat', he built a commanding score of sixty-seven before falling victim to the cruellest of ironies when he played on to his own wicket with a ball that described a complete parabola and hit both wicket and batsman some three seconds after the shot was played.

Right: *Shawcroft and 'that' bat*

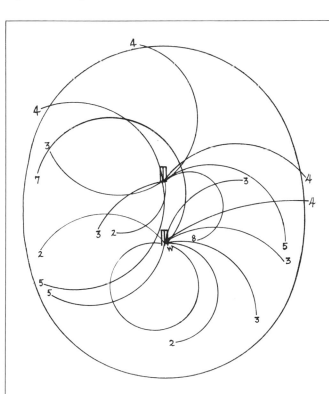

SCORING SEQUENCE

0■ 0 5 0 0 2 0 0 3 0 0 3 0 0
2 2 2 3 0▲ 0 7 4 4 3 5 4 8 4 0
0 0 3 5 5 0 0 ~~1 2 6 7 8~~ 0 0 0
0 0 0 0 2 0 0 3 0 0 W

■ EDGED CATCH BACK TO BOWLER
▲ COVER DRIVES A CATCH TO HIMSELF
W: PLAYED ON VIA LONG LEG

© ARNOLD TURNER

Alex Shawcroft

Among his most remarkable shots was an unforgettable eight which confused the opposing fielders so much that they simply sat down and waited for it to land while he ran on unchallenged for eight runs, and a remarkable seven during which three fielders collided with each other and had to receive medical treatment for amnesia.

It was not, however, the sixty-seven runs that gave the innings its importance, but the fact that the opposing team were so utterly demoralised afterwards that they constantly expected other batsmen to repeat the Shawcroft feat and continued to run around in bemused circles even after cleanly struck straight drives to the boundary.

In all, Shawcroft's effort was to lead to an incredible score of 576 off just thirty overs, or nearly twenty runs an over.

The Shawcroft bat was declared illegal after the match and was destroyed by humane means by the committee of the MCC who examined it at the official enquiry into the whole event. Shawcroft himself did produce a second similar bat later that same season and used it to perform in many celebrity stunts, until a badly cut drive spun around in a vicious ellipse hitting him squarely upon the back of the neck, whereupon he gave up the whole thing and had the last bat chopped into sawdust and donated to the proprietor of a nearby wine lodge.

ASPREY DUKE
(?–1955)

Asprey's great achievement was a phenomenal 'knock' of ninety-three off just thirteen balls whilst playing for a Trinidad and Tobago side against a party of British tourists. The remarkable feat

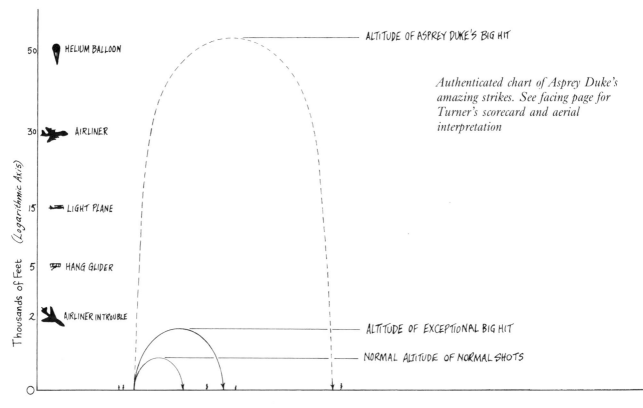

Authenticated chart of Asprey Duke's amazing strikes. See facing page for Turner's scorecard and aerial interpretation

rested almost entirely upon Duke's extraordinary ability to drill the ball directly upwards to quite enormous heights, during which time he would race up and down the length of the wicket while the hapless fielders waited powerless for the ball to return to earth.

Gambling that the chances of catching a ball descending from such an altitude and often covered in ice or snow were minimal, Duke was able to build up a high score with little risk of dismissal. The secret of the Duke technique lay in an enormous pair of shoulders that allowed him to propel the normal cricket ball with such gusto that a shower of sparks and debris was a common accompaniment to most strokes.

Duke's remarkable 'big hit' was eventually brought to an end on the fourteenth ball of his innings when in a display of heroism, four visiting batsmen literally formed a human blanket, lying on the pitch until the ball landed upon one of them and then securing a catch. The method, while solid in principle, did require considerable

```
SCORING  SEQUENCE
5□ 4■ 16# 7† 5✱ 8○ 12ᶻ 10ˣ
4ᵛ 5⁼ 6" 8ᐃ 4▾ W

□DROPPED  ■DROPPED
#DROPPED  †DROPPED  ✱DROPPED
○DROPPED  ᶻDROPPED  ˣDROPPED
ᵛDROPPED  ⁼DROPPED  "DROPPED
ᐃDROPPED  ▾DROPPED  W:CAUGHT
```

© ARNOLD TURNER

Below: *Asprey Duke – the patent method of dismissal. All four fielders arrange themselves in the formation shown, around the point of most likely impact (centre of concentric circles)*

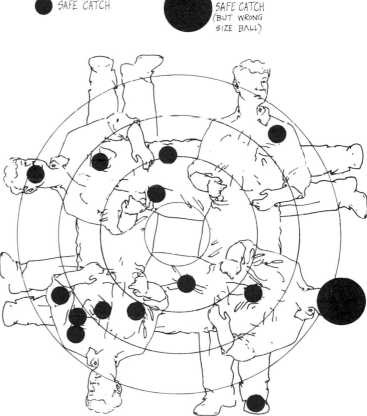

● SAFE CATCH

⬤ SAFE CATCH (BUT WRONG SIZE BALL)

bravery from facing fielders with great risk to their own personal safety. Nonetheless, as other teams adopted the 'human blanket' technique, Duke found his batting average decreased dramatically and eventually was forced to give up his new ploy for more conventional shots.

GARFIELD TWITTY
(1937–   )

A little-known cricketer who had the distinction of scoring 126 not out off a single ball. The incident, not well recorded except in Twitty's native

Right: Garfield Twitty – note the strange home-made wooden wicket so common in much of Tasmanian cricket

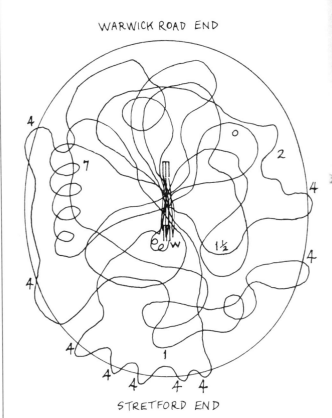

WARWICK ROAD END

STRETFORD END

SCORING SEQUENCE

O O O O O O O O O O O
O O O O O O O O O O O
O O O O O O O 4°4 4 4 4l
4 4 4 4 7 O 2½× O O O O W

°HIT ON HEAD WITH OWN BAT
×INCLUDES 1½ OVERTHROWS
W: STUMPED HIMSELF

© ARNOLD TURNER

Twitty's last innings

Tasmania where it took place, occurred on 9 December, 1961 when Twitty was batting at Number 9 in a local challenge match.

Twitty, whose only previous claim to fame had been to bowl himself out in a vital Sunday League match, achieved his rare honour as a result of imperious bowling. Standing well back to a particularly vicious off-break, Twitty managed to wield his bat in such a way as to actually knock the ball cleanly into his own trouser pocket. Realising what he had done, and not wishing to delay in capitalising upon it, Twitty set off at a furious pace down the wicket, beckoning his fellow-batsman to do likewise. He had scored a remarkable twenty-six before the stricken fielders at last realised what had happened and gave chase. There then followed a remarkable race during which Twitty, hotly pursued by a pack of violent fielders, hared around the perimeter of the pitch, breaking off occasionally to make the odd additional sprint between the wickets and gradually increase his score to 126.

Brought down eventually by a particularly vicious tackle from behind, Twitty was carried off by his fellow team-mates to a hero's welcome. The record still stands today.

CHAPTER NINE

SOME CONTROVERSIAL TEAS

Many are the games that have swung through a vital dismissal, a sturdy innings, or a crucial turn of fate or fortune. Less well chronicled are the great tea intervals that have shaped the history of the game – tea intervals on which matches have been won or lost. Below are recorded those crucial intervals when destiny hung in the balance. Tea intervals like:

THE ASHES TEST OF 1913 AT TRENT BRIDGE

With England all but skittled out in their second innings and their last man in, it would have been a foolish man who would have placed money on an England victory with three hours of play left till stumps were drawn and not a hope of reaching the required total. Yet by skill and judgement the England team were able to keep both their opponents and the umpires locked in the pavilion for a full three hours, thus ensuring a drawn match!

The full history of this truly timeless tea has never emerged but it appears that conspiratorial skills of the highest order were employed to distract umpire and rival players' attention from the proper time and delay their departure from the pavilion till close of play.

The Aussie players were prevented from leaving the pavilion by the heroic though distended bellied England team whose constant requests for

cups and plates to be replenished ensured the Australians, too gallant to refuse, were trapped until it was time to draw stumps.

At the end of this capricious escapade it was estimated that the English players had consumed an average of four gallons of tea per man, and had taken on board a full eight pounds of sugar each. Indeed, even the gross average consumption of sandwiches – at forty-seven rounds per person – was something of a record for the English team. The Australians, forced to witness such gluttony by their opponents, lost all appetite and returned home to Australia a broken, and thinner, team.

The crowd outside the pavilion, on hearing the progress of the gallant English lads within, were held in rapt attention and gave the noble 'tea-timers' (as their team for that Test became known) a rousing cheer at the close of play. Or rather the close of lack of play.

THE CEYLON TEA-TASTING INCIDENT

The Ceylon series 1952. An unfortunate coincidence of the first Test and the local 'tea festival' wreaked utter havoc on play and players alike. By tradition no one may insult the native tea gods by refusing to taste the tea that is offered during this period. And since further tradition requires all visitors to be offered the full 136 blends of native tea it soon became apparent that whatever play was likely to take place was at best only set to be sporadic. In the event, barely had a team taken to the field than they were recalled to the pavilion for more tea. And worse was still to come, for even those few players making the pitch were invariably so sodden with tea that play was quite impossible and a hasty dash back to the nearby latrines was regularly required.

By the close of play on the final day, despite a perfect wicket and cloudless skies, a meagre two hours of play was all that was possible. Curiously, the Australian party who arrived next season and found themselves in the same predicament coped far better. With a national beverage consumption far higher than that of the England team they were able to drink the tea festival dry before going on to bowl their astonished hosts out for a mere twenty-one and thirty-three respectively in their two innings.

THE 1968 TOUR OF CHINA

A somewhat similar affair took place during the Sinhalese tour of China in 1968, a tour designed more as a cultural mission between the two nations than as a cricket series. Each team was insistent that the other partake of its ritualistic tea ceremony, and since one occurred in the late morning and the other in early evening, it transpired that together with the natural mid-afternoon tea interval neither team was on the pitch for more than an hour before a break for tea was required. Indeed the tour rapidly disintegrated into a series of short bursts at the wicket followed by prolonged periods in the pavilion. All matches were naturally drawn and the tea was declared the only winner.

DEXTRY'S LAST TEA
1912

A remarkable tea interval occurred during the last match of the playing career of the illustrious Chamberlaine Dextry, the veteran Worcestershire opener. Determined to better his highest score in this his last match, Dextry found he had reached tea on the last day with a paltry score of twenty-three to his credit, and still facing a target of 194. Aware he was unlikely to succeed by normal methods, he hit upon the novel ploy of duplication and quickly selected eleven supporters from the crowd who most resembled the playing staff of the Gloucestershire opponents he was engaged against. Chancing to notice that both umpires had taken to the wicket early after the interval, and seeing to it that his fellow players realised his trick, he at once took to the field with his bogus opponents and set about destroying the weakly bowling that was deliberately sent down to him.

In a bare eight minutes before the ruse was spotted by his true opponents, Dextry managed to run up a remarkable 140, thus taking his figures to within an ace of the required target. To this end he was helped immensely by a willing crowd who quickly recognised the game afoot and kept deliberately quiet lest they should disturb the Gloucestershire team still resting in the pavilion. Despite protestations by Gloucestershire when they at last discovered the outrage, the umpires admitted it would be easier simply to go on, rather than untangle the mess and the score was allowed to stand with Dextry free to make his record. The fact that he did not do so and was bowled out the very next ball was due mainly to his recent experience with soft bowling which left him totally incapable of offering a shot when a genuine delivery was once again bowled at him.

OLD TRAFFORD
1946

Our final encounter with a remarkable tea interval takes us back to international cricket and an incident less dramatic but every bit as memorable in the study of vital teas. The time is 1946 and at Old Trafford the fifth day of a match between England and a Commonwealth touring party is about to begin. In horror, the backroom staff realise that they have emptied the larder in the previous four days and with rationing still strictly enforced there appears no way of feeding the hungry players upon their return to the pavilion. A frantic search begins and some half-an-hour later two tea bags and an old crust have at last been located and dispatched to the kitchens for a miracle to be performed.

Working feverishly, the kitchen staff do everything they can with the feeble supplies, squeezing, resqueezing and employing every ounce of their culinary skills. At last they are ready and just in time, for at that moment both teams are returning to the pavilion for tea. We need not go into details here; suffice it to say that the result of their culinary guile and genius now displayed before the ravenous players was ... well, was utterly pathetic. One scrap of burnt toast and tea so weak you could add water to it and it would be no less strong. Since that day, cricket has avowed never again to let team catering sink to such a dreadful low. (Needless to say, in the case of spectators' catering, no such vow has ever been taken.)

CHAPTER TEN

PRE-SEASON PRACTICES

As the season draws to an end and a new winter closes in, don't lie idle waiting for next summer to arrive! Use the opportunity of the winter break to polish your skills and swot up on those all-important tactics. I've used this monthly check sheet myself for many years and found it ideal. Try it for yourself!

——October——

Now's the time to stop those rusty joints seizing up. Use this month to keep in trim. Try the exercises once a day and see what a difference they make!

Cricket in winter. This groundsman has devised a clever way of locating the wicket during games of winter cricket

THE 'LIE DOWN'
LIE ON THE FLOOR WITH YOUR FEET ON A PILLOW WITH A PINT OF BEER IN FRONT OF YOU AND SLOWLY SCOOP THE PINT TO YOUR MOUTH AND DRINK FROM IT WITHOUT MOVING.

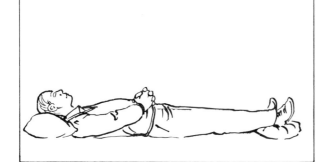

THE 'STAND STILL'
STAND VERY STILL, DON'T DO ANYTHING.

THE 'STAND VERY STILL'
STAND EVEN STILLER AND DO EVEN LESS.

THE 'DO NOTHING'
DO ABSOLUTELY NOTHING ALL DAY, VERY SLOWLY AND REPEAT FOR SEVERAL DAYS.

THE 'SIT STILL'
SIT STILL, VERY STILL, ALL DAY

THE 'PROP UP THE BAR TALKING LOUDLY AND INSULTING FEMALES'

THE 'LIE DOWN IN FRONT OF THE TELLY'
MOVE HAND FORWARD TO ADJUST CONTROLS.

T.V. WITH SOUND TURNED OFF

RADIO 3 TEST MATCH SPECIAL

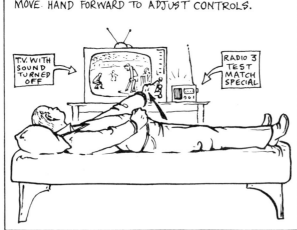

THE 'SIT INSIDE THE CAR ON A BAKING HOT DAY WATCHING OTHER PEOPLE PLAY CRICKET'

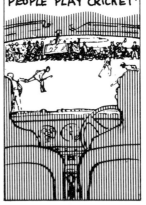

THE 'QUEUEING OUT-SIDE THE BEER TENT FOR HALF AN HOUR DURING A CRICKET MATCH'

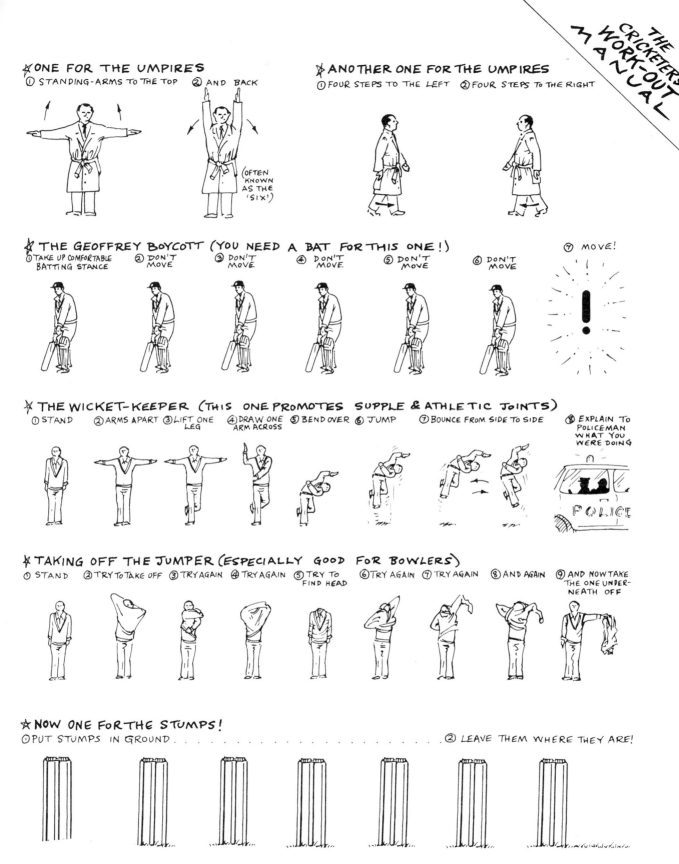

☆ ONE FOR THE UMPIRES
① STANDING—ARMS TO THE TOP ② AND BACK

(OFTEN KNOWN AS THE 'SIX'!)

☆ ANOTHER ONE FOR THE UMPIRES
① FOUR STEPS TO THE LEFT ② FOUR STEPS TO THE RIGHT

☆ THE GEOFFREY BOYCOTT (YOU NEED A BAT FOR THIS ONE!)
① TAKE UP COMFORTABLE BATTING STANCE ② DON'T MOVE ③ DON'T MOVE ④ DON'T MOVE ⑤ DON'T MOVE ⑥ DON'T MOVE ⑦ MOVE!

☆ THE WICKET-KEEPER (THIS ONE PROMOTES SUPPLE & ATHLETIC JOINTS)
① STAND ② ARMS APART ③ LIFT ONE LEG ④ DRAW ONE ARM ACROSS ⑤ BEND OVER ⑥ JUMP ⑦ BOUNCE FROM SIDE TO SIDE ⑧ EXPLAIN TO POLICEMAN WHAT YOU WERE DOING

POLICE

☆ TAKING OFF THE JUMPER (ESPECIALLY GOOD FOR BOWLERS)
① STAND ② TRY TO TAKE OFF ③ TRY AGAIN ④ TRY AGAIN ⑤ TRY TO FIND HEAD ⑥ TRY AGAIN ⑦ TRY AGAIN ⑧ AND AGAIN ⑨ AND NOW TAKE THE ONE UNDERNEATH OFF

☆ NOW ONE FOR THE STUMPS!
① PUT STUMPS IN GROUND . . . . ② LEAVE THEM WHERE THEY ARE!

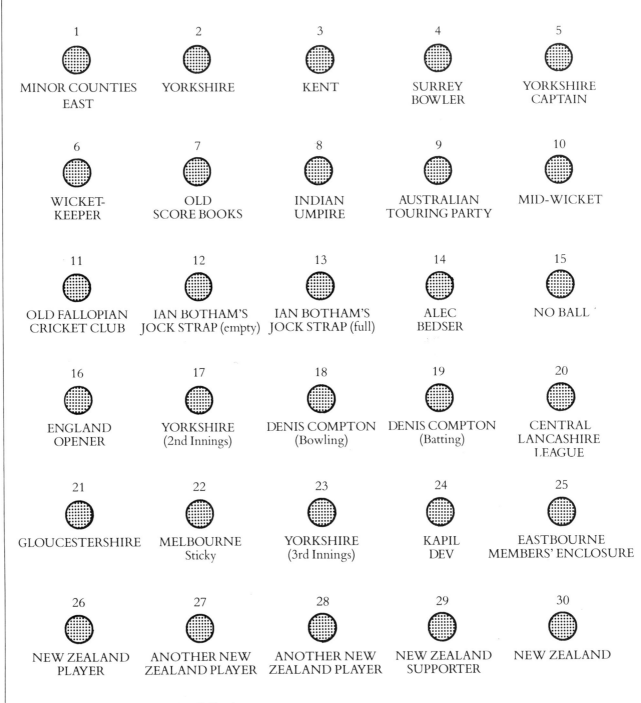

1 MINOR COUNTIES EAST

2 YORKSHIRE

3 KENT

4 SURREY BOWLER

5 YORKSHIRE CAPTAIN

6 WICKET-KEEPER

7 OLD SCORE BOOKS

8 INDIAN UMPIRE

9 AUSTRALIAN TOURING PARTY

10 MID-WICKET

11 OLD FALLOPIAN CRICKET CLUB

12 IAN BOTHAM'S JOCK STRAP (empty)

13 IAN BOTHAM'S JOCK STRAP (full)

14 ALEC BEDSER

15 NO BALL

16 ENGLAND OPENER

17 YORKSHIRE (2nd Innings)

18 DENIS COMPTON (Bowling)

19 DENIS COMPTON (Batting)

20 CENTRAL LANCASHIRE LEAGUE

21 GLOUCESTERSHIRE

22 MELBOURNE Sticky

23 YORKSHIRE (3rd Innings)

24 KAPIL DEV

25 EASTBOURNE MEMBERS' ENCLOSURE

26 NEW ZEALAND PLAYER

27 ANOTHER NEW ZEALAND PLAYER

28 ANOTHER NEW ZEALAND PLAYER

29 NEW ZEALAND SUPPORTER

30 NEW ZEALAND

Cricketers' Scratch 'n' Sniff Card
Simply scratch the dot to receive the cricketing smells indicated

November

Keep alive your cricketing interests this month with the Cricketers' Scratch 'n' Sniff card. One scratch for each day of the month. By the end you should have the most alert cricket nose this side of Brian Johnston. (*See facing page*).

December

Revision this month!

With nets not far away now, this is the time to bone up on those cricketing tactics you slipped up on last term. Like . . . the toss! Use the month of December to brush up on your abilities as a tosser.

A SHORT HISTORY OF THE TOSS

How did the practice of tossing to select which team hits first evolve? It is a question often asked. More important, what advice should be given to the young cricketer called in to take part in this most difficult of tasks? Let us see if we can shed some light on both fronts.

The practice of tossing up, or tossing off as it was previously called, began in the early years of this century as a way to avoid the arguments and confrontations that regularly occurred at the start of a match. Often both teams would signal their intent to take the field and would not be dissuaded from this end by the other side's protestations. There would then follow a prolonged period of argument, with both captains refusing to give way on the issue and adamant in their determination to bat first – or last, whichever was the more attractive.

Occasionally, and with horrific results, both teams would elect to bat and four batsmen would then take to the field and no bowlers. Or worse still, twenty players would find themselves in fielding positions on the pitch with two opening bowlers at opposite ends of the ground preparing to let fly at each other.

It was clear to all that some process of determining the correct order of innings should be found before serious carnage resulted and to this end the authorities considered a large number of worthy suggestions. Straws were used for a short period, as too were playing cards, and even, in one case, a dramatic car race around the edge of the field. The practice of who could hold his breath the longest was used on one occasion only. Both captains were proud men and only after the interval on the second day was it revealed that rather than let their team down both had tragically died of asphyxiation. The memorial poem 'There's a Breathless Hush in the Close Tonight' is well known.

Quizzes and tests of endurance were popular for a short while but the length of time they took precluded their use in all but long or drawn-out matches where one could afford the luxury of losing an entire day's play simply to settle the matter of who should bat first.

And so came the decision to throw or 'toss' a coin in the air – the idea coming, so it is said, from one captain's furious pledge that he 'couldn't give a toss who batted first', thereby suggesting to the opposite captain the use of a coin. From that day, the use of the coin has remained largely unchallenged, apart from a brief period in the early part of the century when in an effort to ascertain complete fairness in any adjudication, the idea of tossing up to see who should call when the *actual* toss was made, was suggested, developing to the point where a separate toss was made to see who should call when the toss that was made to see who should call when the toss was made, was made.

Normally, in the tossing of a coin, the coin is allowed to come to rest on the upturned hand of the umpire or an impartial adviser, but where a hand is not available, or where that which is available is considered unsuitable for reasons of hygiene, the coin may instead be allowed to fall to the floor. On no account should the coin be allowed to fall more than a distance considered reasonable to secure a fair and unbiased choice. In some early cases, umpires have attempted to increase the appearance of fairness by dropping the coin from the top of a tall building and have been faced with an arduous walk up and then down five or six storeys to see what face of the coin is showing, only to find that they are exhausted and totally unable to perform their normal duties on the field. Or, as on one recorded occasion, that someone had stolen the coin.

The toss should always be carried out with speed and authority. Never delay telling the captain what the coin shows. Examples of an umpire refusing to tell either captain the outcome because 'it is a secret' are not unknown. So too are cases of the umpire refusing point blank to tell the captain what the true result is till he, the umpire, has been told 'what it is worth'. At all costs, umpires should refrain from giving false or misleading suggestions by the use of a sarcastic or disparaging tone, as in 'well, it's not heads anyway'.

The umpire should resist all attempts by the losing captain to make it double or quits, or to make it the best out of three. He should also refuse to allow himself to be crossed with holy water before making a toss or cursed by the gods of voodoo, as has occurred during some tours of far-flung corners of the Empire.

The Science of the Toss

With the introduction of the toss came also the science of tossology: the attempt to predict the correct way a coin would land. The first student to investigate the science in detail was Freigal whose work (*Science In The Toss Of A Coin*, Lisbon, 1916) contains the now famous equation:

$$a + ab + q^2 - rx^4 + (345 \div \frac{xyz}{p})^4 + a^5 = a^2 b^3 (x + yz^0)\frac{pq}{0}$$

Working on Freigal's equation, some captains enjoyed a modicum of success, notably Fraterni,

the captain of Wiltshire, who in 1922 predicted the toss of a coin correctly on two occasions, so he claimed, on the basis of the equation. However, in 1924 Leibina was able to prove Freigal wrong with his own classic theorem:

$$(\alpha + \beta)^2 + (8 + x + y + pq^2)^2 + 1 = \frac{a + b + c + d}{(46 + xy(z))}$$

which stated that if the third quotient of the binary exponent of the root was exceeded on any one toss, then the function would exceed the mathematical mean of maximum curvature.

In 1936 three years' research by Hollroyd into the work of both Freigal and Leibina culminated in proving a causal linkage between the heat pressure gradient of the locally induced environment, allied to a low value delta score which he attributed to the state of the tosser's thumb. British and American scientists worked together on the same problem in 1943 and were able to confirm Hollroyd's experimental findings while measuring the effect of tossing the coin at temperatures as low as -200°C.

Their work, *Clinico-kinetic Research in the Trajectory of Coinage* (Nevada, 1943), proved the startling gnomic theorem that if a certain coin is tossed by a certain captain, then it will consistently land on the opposite side to that predicted provided the person making that choice is the captain of the England XI.

Baibol in 1952 was able to identify the 'gnomic' factor more closely when he studied the effect of tossing the same coin two-and-a-half million times under strict laboratory conditions. He published his research paper, *Alpha Tharg in M-units in the Critical Path Analysis of Travel* (MacCintney University, 1952) and was quickly to see his theory validated by a Tomjchevski paper to the Moscow Academy for the Advancement of Science (Cricket Faculty) in 1954.

Papers by Norme (1958) and Toadsley (1961) seemed to bear out this theory, until a quite remarkable study by Collinge and Jones of the University of New South Wales (Department of

Theoretical Cricket), which stated in simple terms that:

$$\frac{a + an + dhg + shd^2 + 565ngm^{666} + dhf^5 + snhd^{34524353}}{543 - snd^{444} - mnd^6 + kjhd \times \left(\dfrac{msn^6 + sndh + sdg\,(34)}{ans^0 + 34b(a) - \dfrac{y(n)}{100}}\right)} = 0$$

This confounded the critics and it wasn't until 1974 that Billinge and Billinge, working with laserscan and sound spectrum analysis, were able to develop a random-aggregate theory that allowed a correct prediction of 63 per cent of calls. Clearly a radical breakthrough, the Billinge and Billinge technique relied on computer ordnance vacuum analysis with a series of complex laboratory simulations of the tosser's left arm. These, together with the multi-spectral oscillations, took a full three days to assimilate and while with practice Billinge and Billinge hope to reduce the period to perhaps two-and-a-half days, it remains too long for the normal cricket captain, who has perhaps just a matter of seconds to make his call.

Postscript

In 1985 it was learnt that the Russian Space Agency had perfected a way of successfully predicting the outcome of 71.3 per cent of all calls made when a coin was tossed in an orbiting space station, and it was felt that within the near future this figure could reach something like 72 or even 73 per cent. The disadvantage is that laboratory conditions must be maintained requiring the complete and sole use of an orbiting space station for twelve years, and a computer bigger than all existing computers combined.

At present the Russians have resisted this development despite pressure from several cricketing authorities, and a promise by Britain to provide the coin.

English Test Matches:

The result of England toss-up calls since 1870 (in chronological order)

LOST LOST LOST LOST LOST LOST LOST LOST

LOST LOST LOST LOST LOST LOST LOST LOST

LOST LOST LOST LOST LOST LOST LOST LOST

LOST LOST LOST LOST LOST LOST LOST LOST

LOST LOST LOST LOST LOST LOST LOST LOST

LOST LOST LOST LOST LOST LOST LOST LOST

LOST LOST LOST LOST LOST LOST LOST LOST

LOST LOST LOST LOST LOST LOST LOST LOST

LOST LOST LOST LOST WON LOST LOST LOST

LOST LOST LOST LOST LOST LOST LOST LOST

LOST LOST LOST LOST LOST LOST LOST LOST

LOST LOST LOST LOST LOST LOST LOST LOST

LOST LOST DREW LOST LOST LOST LOST LOST

LOST LOST LOST LOST LOST LOST LOST LOST

LOST LOST LOST LOST LOST LOST LOST LOST

LOST LOST LOST WON (LOST ON RE-COUNT) LOST

LOST LOST LOST LOST LOST LOST LOST LOST

LOST LOST LOST LOST LOST LOST LOST LOST

LOST LOST LOST LOST LOST LOST LOST LOST

LOST LOST LOST LOST LOST LOST LOST LOST

LOST LOST LOST LOST LOST LOST LOST WON

LOST LOST LOST LOST LOST LOST LOST LOST

LOST LOST LOST LOST LOST LOST LOST LOST

LOST LOST LOST LOST LOST LOST LOST LOST

LOST LOST LOST LOST LOST LOST LOST LOST

LOST LOST LOST LOST LOST LOST LOST LOST

January

FOR YOUR PROTECTION

Now is the time to check on your jock-strap. Especially if you naven't removed it since September. Make sure it is well oiled and greased and ready for the new season. Check that you know the rules regarding the use of the jock-strap that we reprint here. More advanced readers may care to do some background reading on other protective garments that have been used.

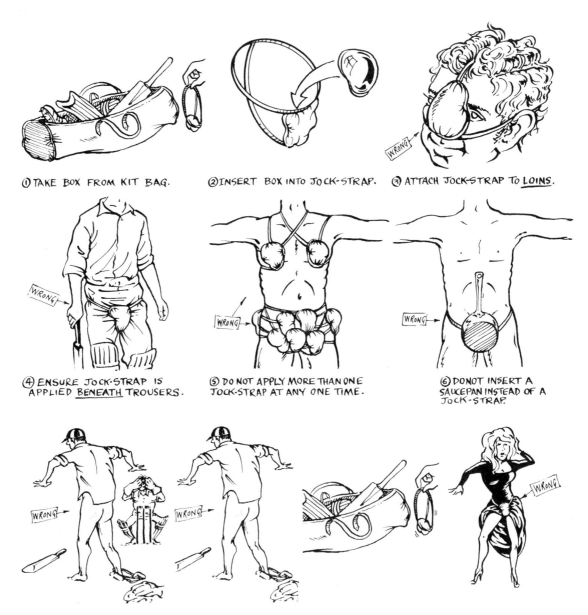

① TAKE BOX FROM KIT BAG.

② INSERT BOX INTO JOCK-STRAP.

③ ATTACH JOCK-STRAP TO LOINS.

④ ENSURE JOCK-STRAP IS APPLIED BENEATH TROUSERS.

⑤ DO NOT APPLY MORE THAN ONE JOCK-STRAP AT ANY ONE TIME.

⑥ DO NOT INSERT A SAUCEPAN INSTEAD OF A JOCK-STRAP.

⑦ IF THE JOCK-STRAP BECOMES DETACHED DURING PLAY, DO NOT REMOVE TROUSERS TO INVESTIGATE.

⑧ DO NOT REMOVE TROUSERS FOR ANY OTHER REASON EITHER.

⑨ ALWAYS REMOVE YOUR OWN (BUT NO ONE ELSE'S) JOCK-STRAP AFTER LEAVING THE FIELD OF PLAY & REPLACE IN KIT BAG.

⑩ NEVER OFFER YOUR JOCK-STRAP TO A LADY. ESPECIALLY IF YOU ARE WEARING IT AT THE TIME.

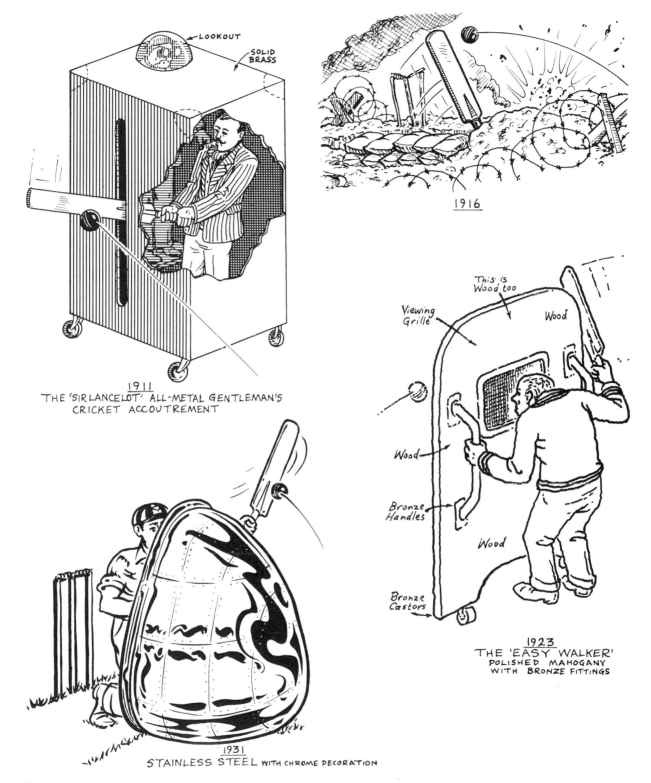

LOOKOUT

SOLID BRASS

1911
THE 'SIR LANCELOT' ALL-METAL GENTLEMAN'S CRICKET ACCOUTREMENT

1916

This is Wood too

Viewing Grille

Wood

Wood

Bronze Handles

Wood

Bronze Castors

1923
THE 'EASY WALKER' POLISHED MAHOGANY WITH BRONZE FITTINGS

1931
STAINLESS STEEL WITH CHROME DECORATION

Cricket protection through the ages

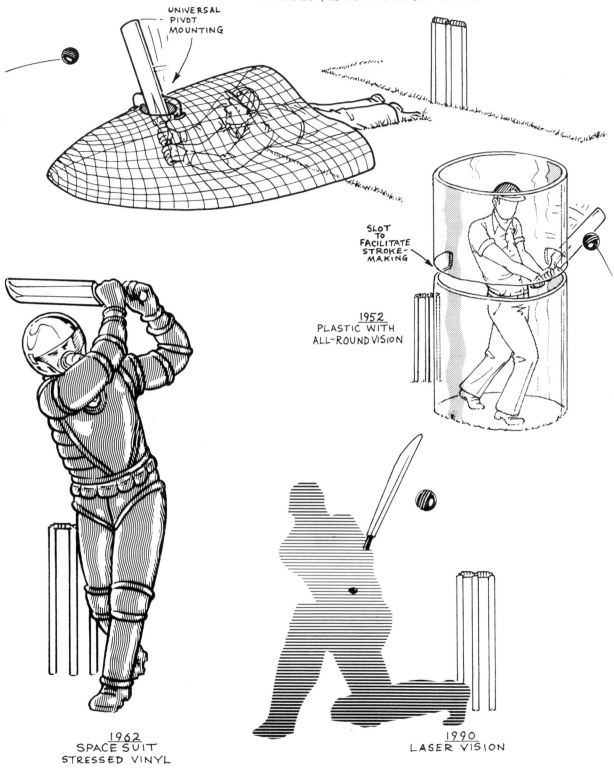

1937
WIRE MESH, AERODYNAMICALLY SHAPED

UNIVERSAL PIVOT MOUNTING

SLOT TO FACILITATE STROKE-MAKING

1952
PLASTIC WITH ALL-ROUND VISION

1962
SPACE SUIT
STRESSED VINYL

1990
LASER VISION

More cricket protection through the ages

February

More revision. Time to 'gen up' on cricket supporters ready for the months ahead.

THE SUPPORTER

The MCC type His watch stopped in 1952. Continually surprised to find there are people who play the game for money. Asks why we haven't seen the South Africans over here recently. Advises all young players to take a straight bat to everything, especially if it wears a skirt and talks too much. Sits in a row with fifty identical supporters.

Yorkshire – Or Alternative MCC – Male Chauvinist Cricketer Will have an obstinate sense of obstinacy. Unlikely to see the other man's point of view. Unless the other man is from Yorkshire and has exactly the same point of view as himself. Will know all there is to know about all there is to know. Idea of a good day is a day spent talking to no one at a club annual general meeting. Blunt, abrupt, plain-spoken and sharp-tongued. And that is when he is being pleasant. Married, but can't remember why. Hopes to live in Yorkshire for the rest of his life. We hope he does too.

Australian His idea of a perfect cricketer is someone who can drink, swear, pull women and upset people more than himself. Cricketing ability is not important. Believes that cricket is an assertion of manhood and that the cricket bat when taken out to the wicket is a phallic symbol of male authority. Sees his role of supporter as a way of enforcing this. Enjoys anything that doesn't involve propriety. Regards crying by a team captain as a criminal offence. Deplores the recent bout of sportsmanship between English and Australian teams.

West Indian Warm and good natured, the West Indians have become so accustomed to victory that the possibility of defeat has been removed from their psyche. They pay little attention to the result of their team's match and more to the manner in which that result is achieved. Psychologists, aware of the effect a humiliating defeat might have on the West Indian community, have long recommended counselling centres ready to take the victims if such a blow should occur. It is estimated that a normal, well-balanced, West Indian supporter faced with a crushing defeat might take up to five years to get over the shock. I do hope my warnings are not ignored. The West Indian supporter in England, especially that one with the tin can, has the most appalling sense of rhythm.

Sponsor's guest There is a new type of supporter who would not normally be seen dead at a cricket match. He is invited by a sponsor to sit in a sweaty tent, drink champagne and go through the motions of watching the game by glancing at a television set every two or three hours. This is fine in itself until one of their number in the mistaken belief that he should actually watch a bit of the cricket wanders out and gives the players a few words of encouragement, *viz.* the shouting of 'What a load of rubbish', 'Ar-se-nal' and 'Come on, Botham, you great fairy, hit 'em for seven' – all of which, though well meant, does little to solve the problem of inner city riots.

March

HOW TO INSPECT A WICKET

More practical activities ahead as the new season looms large. First start by inspecting that there is a pitch. This is especially important in agricultural communities where many pitches may all but disappear after the winter break. It is also important if contemplating a game in winter when there is snow on the ground.

When you have found your pitch, or what appears to be a pitch, look for an area of shorter grass in the middle. If there is an area of longer grass in the middle you should consult the groundsman. If you cannot find the groundsman check in the area of longer grass to see if he is hiding there.

Provided you have found the area of shorter grass, (i.e. the wicket) start a careful inspection for lumps, bumps or divots. It is often a good idea to make out a simple diagram for yourself like this with the bumps marked:

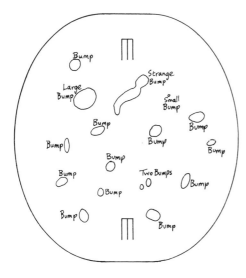

Here is another example:

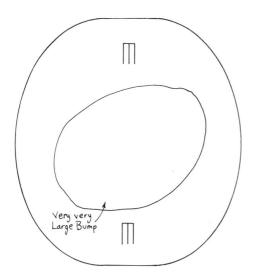

You should measure the bumps by size. A bump the size of a fist is small. A bump the size of a football is large. A bump the size of a man is probably the groundsman you couldn't find earlier.

Try and see which way the pitch runs. Does it have a gradient? A short walk will normally tell you this. If you find yourself moving at speed and unable to stop, this means the pitch has a very sharp gradient. Look for any changes in gradient. Make a drawing of what you find. Some examples are shown opposite.

Now look at the texture and feel of the surface. Is it wet or dry? If you find yourself *floating* it is probably moist. Or it is probably not quite the same sort of grass that you thought it was. Try and study the type of grass. *Do be specific:* it is no use to your plans simply writing down 'short green stuff that comes out of the ground'. Look for patches of bare earth. Do not try and count the number of blades of grass. This is not important.

ADVANCED PITCH INSPECTION

Advanced inspection is required for important games. It is also useful for minor games when you wish to upset or unnerve your opponents.

Gradient Competent professional survey and reconnaissance firms can provide a full geodetic survey of any pitch you require. They will need several days to complete the work and may need to make several holes in the pitch if you require seismic reports for the geological strata below a depth of 2000 feet. This information may be useful if you lose the actual match and want to start looking for oil instead. Remember geologists should not encroach on to the pitch during a match without both captains' permission. On no account should geologists erect drilling wells in the centre of the crease during an important match.

Moisture Nowadays moisture measurers are widely available (Packer Products Ltd, Alice and Sheila Springs, Australia, allow four to six years

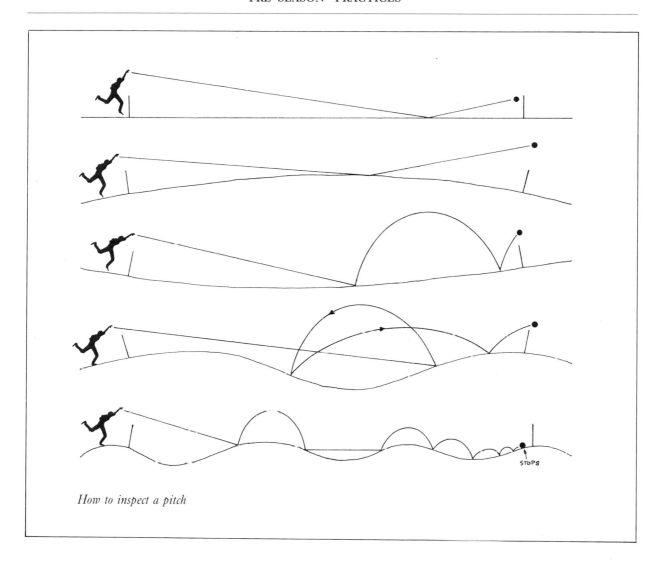

How to inspect a pitch

for delivery). The tip of the instrument is inserted in the top layer of soil for an instant reading. No one knows what the reading means but at least it's instant.

Grass To measure the depth of grass insert the RANCO ALL-ELECTRICAL GRASS MEASURE (£9.95, batteries not included, the ideal Christmas present) and wait for the electric buzzer to give you not only the size of the grass but also the temperature, the humidity, the time, your birthday, and the capital city of Venezuela.

Ambient Atmosphere Temperature, humidity and condensation level can be measured using the RANCO HUMIDITY RECORDER – a unique fur-lined balaclava helmet. Put it on your head. If you sweat inside ten seconds it means it's hot. Inside five seconds means it's very hot. Inside two seconds (plus difficulty in breathing) means either you're on fire or you've put it on the wrong way round. (Batteries are not included.)

[75]

April

One month to go! Use it to make sure you know these all-important cricketing terms.

Silly Midriff	The gap between a player's shirt and pants in a local Sunday league match.
Square Head	Haircut given to Australian opening batsmen.
Square Cut	(See Square Head above.)
Thick Point	Any suggestion treated with contempt by fellow players.
Ticklish Edge	Part of the anatomy that causes irritation when fielding (see Silly Midriff).
Deep Long Sticky	(See Ticklish Edge.)
Yorkshire	Type of cricket played by a team without a recognised captain.
Silly Toss	Player who manages to get himself out for no reason.
One-day Match	A match of any nominal length which involves the West Indies.
Leg Break	What usually happens when a cricket ball strikes you on the shin when fielding.
Short Stumps	Jocular Australian expression used to express contempt at a fellow player's lack of height.
No Crease	Type of trouser worn by local league cricketer.
Wide Leg	Type of trouser worn by person with fat legs (also used by a player who attempts to explain a dubious lbw decision).
Slips	Name given to fielding technique in wet conditions.
Short Deep Wicket	A wicket placed deep into the ground and therefore shorter than the other wickets.
Short Leg	The effect of wearing the wrong trousers.
Nightwatchman	One who goes in late at night with a view to scoring more runs and staying far longer than the recognised batsmen.

CHAPTER ELEVEN

THE SELECTOR CALLS

A play in one act for cricketers

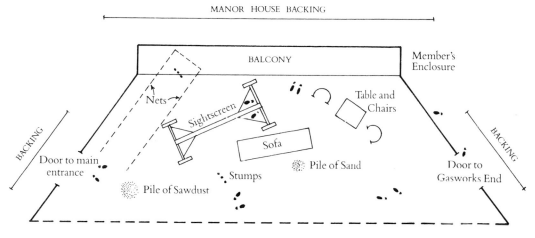

First presented by H.M. Tennant in association with I. Zingari Productions Ltd at the Old Vic, London, on the 13th of April, 1948, with the following cast of characters –

Inspector	Richard Attenborough
Lady Maltravers	Denis Compton*
Cook	Irene Handl
Jeavons, the Butler	E. W. Swanton
Lady Primhouse	Brian Close
Forlorn, the Gardener	John Gielgud‡
Dead Body	Trevor Bailey

Cigarettes by Abdullah
Whiter-Than-Whites by Mrs Benaud's Chinese Laundry
Stockings by Kray Twins [Stepney and England]

The play is directed by Sir Stafford Cripps
Setting Alec Bedser   Stumps drawn by Margaret Lockwood

The action takes place on a wet Thursday a day before the start of the last Test

*Matinees only   ‡Wicketkeeper

A short drinks interval takes place between acts

SCENE 1

The hallway of Maltravers Hall. Lady Maltravers and Jeavons the faithful butler stand at the foot of the stairs. The hallway is most elegantly fashioned in the furnishings of the day. A short passage leads off left. There is a knock at the door. . . .

LADY MALTRAVERS: (*Moving swiftly to leg*) I'll answer it. (*She opens the door to find a tall well-dressed man waiting on the doorstep.*) Yes?

MAN (INSPECTOR): You called?

LADY MALTRAVERS (NOT OUT): Inspector! I'm sorry I didn't recognise you, please come in. . . .

[The Inspector enters the hallway and nods cordially to the other guests. He removes his hat and coat and we see he is wearing full cricket flannels and pads. In one hand he carries a bat.]

INSPECTOR: Please forgive me, your ladyship – I was playing cricket when I received your call and I didn't have time to change. . . .

LADY MALTRAVERS: Not at all, Inspector.

INSPECTOR: Pay no attention to my dress – I assure you it will make not a shred of difference to my solving this case. Now where is the body?

LADY MALTRAVERS: Through here, Inspector. . . .

[The Inspector points the way into the drawing-room, her ladyship nods . . . the others present follow on.]

INSPECTOR: (*Surveying scene*) Cook – I want you to go square of point to cut off the quick single. Jeavons, we need you to cover the window in case he goes for the hook clear of cover. Lady Primhouse, I want you square between gully and mid-on, again to cut off the short single. Forlorn, you take second slip. You, Lady Maltravers, will take the stumper's job, and I will bowl. . . . Now, tell me all you know of the crime.

[The guests take their respective positions uneasily.]

LADY MALTRAVERS: Inspector, are you sure you wouldn't like a drink to take your mind off the cricket?

INSPECTOR: No, Lady Maltravers – cricket is the last thing on my mind I assure you. Now where is the body?

LADY MALTRAVERS: (*Leading the way to the corner of the room where lies the dead body of a young man.*) Over here, Inspector.

INSPECTOR: (*Checking the body*) I see, middle and leg, where's the cricket ball?

LADY MALTRAVERS: Cricket ball, Inspector?

INSPECTOR: Yes, the cricket ball that killed him.

LADY MALTRAVERS: He was stabbed, Inspector.

INSPECTOR: Stabbed by a cricket ball? How interesting.

LADY MALTRAVERS: No, Inspector, by a knife. . . .

INSPECTOR: I see, but why should anyone be playing cricket with a knife?

LADY MALTRAVERS: They weren't, Inspector.

INSPECTOR: Then you admit you lied to me.

LADY MALTRAVERS: No, Inspector – they weren't playing cricket with a knife. . . .

INSPECTOR: This is proving more difficult to fathom than I first assumed. Cook, what do you know of all this?

COOK: Please, Inspector – the first I knew was when the mistress came in and said the young master had been stabbed, sir. . . .

INSPECTOR: I see, and where were you fielding when this happened?

COOK: Beg pardon, sir. . . .

INSPECTOR: Come on, where were you fielding, it's a simple enough question. . . .

COOK: Fielding, Inspector?

INSPECTOR: Which *position*? Where were you positioned?

COOK: Please, sir, I wasn't fielding.

INSPECTOR: Then you were batting. . . .

COOK: No, Inspector.

INSPECTOR: Aha – you were waiting to bat?

COOK: (*After much thought*) No, Inspector.

INSPECTOR: Then I fail to see what it was you were doing here?

COOK: If it please, Inspector, I was making tea.

INSPECTOR: Aha – I see – for the interval.

COOK: Er . . . what interval?

INSPECTOR: The tea interval of course! Are you stupid, woman . . .?

COOK: No, Inspector, there wasn't no interval.

INSPECTOR: (*Striding thoughtfully around room, exercising arm in preparation for bowling.*) Then if you weren't making tea for the interval, what were you making it for?

COOK: (*Sobbing*) Please, Inspector, I haven't done nothing, I don't know what you're saying these things to me for. . . .

[*The Inspector takes down a cricket bat that happens to be hanging on the wall and starts to tap the corpse with the end of it rather as a batsman might at the start of his innings.*]

INSPECTOR:	All right butler, crowd in a little around the batsmen (*the butler closes in*). Where were you when the murder was committed?
BUTLER:	In my quarters, Inspector.
INSPECTOR:	(*Eyeing him with suspicion*) In your quarters eh?
BUTLER:	Yes, Inspector.
INSPECTOR:	In pads?
BUTLER:	What?
INSPECTOR:	Were you wearing pads?
BUTLER:	No, Inspector.
INSPECTOR:	I see – you weren't wearing pads – even though you knew that in a very short while you would be called upon to bat?
BUTLER:	What?
INSPECTOR:	Just answer the question, that is all!
BUTLER:	(*He is lost for words, stares blankly.*)
INSPECTOR:	Yes, I thought I'd catch you out. Well, what have you got to say?
BUTLER:	Please, Inspector, I haven't the faintest idea what you're talking about. . . .
INSPECTOR:	(*Makes a few trial sprints up and down the wicket as a bowler preparing before a spell of overs.*) All right, butler, wait over by long leg. I wish to speak to the gardener – over here, man. . . .

[*The gardener approaches; as he does so the Inspector tosses an imaginary cricket ball at him . . . the gardener, uncertain of what he should do, makes a weak and half-hearted effort to catch the ball. . . .*]

INSPECTOR:	All right, pick it up later. Now we have the cook's and the butler's confessions, but what about you, eh? What d'you have to say for yourself, so-called gardener?
GARDENER:	I don't know what you mean.
INSPECTOR:	All right, let me put it this way then – a medium-pace seam bowler, five wickets down, five to fall, the ball is turning but not much. He has five men to leg and three to off. He can continue to bowl a full length hoping for one to turn, or. . . .
GARDENER:	Or, Inspector?
INSPECTOR:	Or what else can he do?
GARDENER:	I don't know, Inspector.
INSPECTOR:	Don't know . . . or don't want to know?
GARDENER:	I haven't a clue what you're talking about.
INSPECTOR:	So you deny it ever happened!
GARDENER:	Deny what ever happened happened?
INSPECTOR:	Whatever did happen . . . little less square please your ladyship. . . .

GARDENER:	I haven't done anything. . . .
INSPECTOR:	Exactly. I put it to you, so-called gardener, that you would have been prepared to continue with the same field without even considering a quicker ball to leg to catch the man with a sharp edge?
GARDENER:	I don't know what you mean.
INSPECTOR:	Yes, I thought I'd catch you out eventually . . . and you Lady Maltravers – what of you?
LADY MALTRAVERS:	Oh God, I can't stand this nonsense any longer. All right, I admit I did it . . . I killed the young man who is really my father's illegitimate son who stood to inherit the fortune that was rightfully mine but which he knew I would lose were he able to expose my relationship with the evil Lord Balfont whose estate had been misappropriated from the ageing Duke De Cavelot without his knowledge and which therefore left me prey to blackmail. I had to kill him . . . he would have ruined me, don't you see . . . but you won't have the satisfaction of taking me alive . . . for I have a knife and I am prepared to use it . . . arghhhhhhhh.

[*She stabs herself through the heart, collapsing dead. . . . The others rush over to help Lady Maltravers but too late. The Inspector taps the body lightly with the cricket bat trying to pat her down as would a batsman patting down a lump on the pitch.*]

INSPECTOR:	Right, well, who's going to open the bowling, now then?

END OF SCENE 1

SCENE 2

The morning room, same day. Jeavons is by the window alongside the Inspector. To the left cook approaches nervously. Square of cook covering gully stands Lady Primhouse, a weekend guest of the Maltraverses. In the deep, past mid-wicket, stands Forlorn the gardener looking for a thick edge. Lord Maltravers approaches with the sightscreen.

ALL:	'Owzat!

THE END

CHAPTER TWELVE

BRIGHTER CRICKET

THE true cricket lover finds it almost inconceivable that there could be anything brighter than cricket, and that anything designed to make it more exciting still would cause so many heart attacks that such sports as motor racing, boxing and rock-climbing would be ever-more regarded as cissy by comparison. However, with the advent of sponsorship, more was requested by the tobacco and life assurance companies. To this end, in 1981, the First International Committee For Brighter Cricket met in Scarborough for an intensive weekend school looking at ways of 'improving' the game. Unfortunately the only copy of that committee's findings was lost in the train on the way home. By interviewing all but two of the committee members I have managed to produce a summary. The committee considered the following alternative rules.

TIP-AND-RUN

The first international tip-and-run match was held at Llayallpunji in August 1953, when England easily defeated an all-India (and some bits of Tibet) side, due mainly to some excellent tipping by Ronald Bagstaffe, perhaps the finest tipper England has ever produced. Two years later the Australians sent a team to play England in a three-match series. The England team again won easily because as everyone knows Australians are terrible tippers. Since then the game has not been revived. Memorable English tippers have been Rodney Tipshaw, who tipped for England many

times at amateur level, receiving a tipping blue at Cambridge, and the British Leyland School, who have produced many excellent tippers.

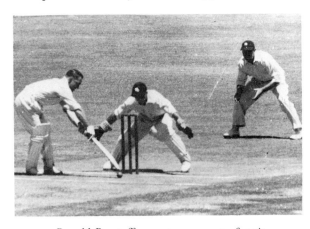

Ronald Bagstaffe executes a near-perfect tip

SIX-AND-OUT

(*Originally called Sex and Out due to a typing error, which led to the controversial though very popular English Sex and Out Tour of the West Indies in 1938*) The only full Test to be played under full six-and-out rules took place in July 1948, when South Africa played England at Cape Town. The game proved singularly disappointing. Both teams bowled slow left arm around the wicket to tempt the opponents into rash or foolish shots that would see them score the necessary six for a dismissal. However, the batsmen simply took the opportunity to drive the deliveries along the ground for a series of fours, never once being tempted to go for the big hit skywards. Even calls from the spectators of 'I bet he'll hit a really incredible six off the next ball' and 'I really admire the way he opens his shoulders up and goes for the big hit' failed to encourage either team to hit the ball high. At the end of play, England were 971 for 0 declared in their first innings and 1640 for 0 in the second, whilst South Africa were 874 for 0 in their first innings and 974 for 0 in the second. The match was drawn.

FRENCH CRICKET

Several county sides played a form of French cricket until the 1950s. Most successful were Glamorgan, who won the Gauloise Cup Competition for French cricket in 1931 and again in 1935 and 1936. Unfortunately, the post-war years saw a far more aggressive spate of bowling by French cricket bowlers that eroded the charm the game had previously enjoyed. Several players were hospitalised after facing full-toss deliveries from two or three yards out, while several bowlers were alarmed to discover batsmen hooking nice soft deliveries down the throats of waiting fielders. Perhaps the worst of all incidents occurred when Lancashire played Nottinghamshire in a tense match and the Notts captain was mercilessly felled by a yorker bowled at the backs of his shins from two feet away. No major counties play French cricket now, although in recent seasons England touring teams have attempted to introduce many tactics from French cricket into Test Matches.

PEA ROLLERS
(and underarm bowling)

Remarkably few first-class bowlers bowl underarm in English cricket today. England has not produced a fine fast underarm bowler for over 120 years – this despite its obvious advantages on unpredictable or rough wickets where a craftily bowled pea roller at the end of a spell of conven-

tional bowling has long been recognised as a successful ploy. In 1864, the last year of widespread underarm bowling in Britain, the Minor Counties East captain, Crowthorns, took no less than 340 wickets in one season, his trick being to aim for the batsmen's toes with alarming skill and alacrity.

Opinion differs as to why underarm bowling went into such a state of decline, the more likely explanation being the modern cricketer's own self-discipline and his reluctance to reduce what is supposed to be a manly sport to a giant game of marbles. Underarm bowling is still permissible in the rules.

ONE-HANDED BATTING

One-handed batting is usually adopted when one player hopelessly outclasses his opponents and some form of handicapping is required (as for instance with West Indian players against anyone).

One-handed batting is also adopted when the batsman has anything less than two hands.

FREE WICKET

Little used in cricket, a free wicket is sometimes awarded for a misdemeanour but it never made the transition from beach cricket to ordinary cricket that some had predicted. The alternative ruling – *free bat*, where the batsman is allowed to defend his wicket, the only restriction being that his bat is taken away – was briefly popular in the Lancashire League in the 1906 season, although a sickening number of head injuries to gallant batsmen intent on keeping their wickets intact at all costs quickly put paid to the habit. (Incidentally, the *free ball*, under which ruling the batsman is allowed to hit a stationary ball placed on the ground in front of him, later went on to become the game of golf, hence the golfing expression 'fore!' borrowed from cricket; 'Watch out, I'm going to hit a four!')

THE COMMITTEE'S FINDINGS

The committee decided that as none of these ideas had proved successful in the past there was no point in reviving them now. They noted, however, that some of the more dangerous aspects (e.g. the sickening head injuries caused by the free bat rule) had definite possibilities and could be adopted at a later date.

Some *new* ideas were also considered.

HANDICAPPING

A handicapping system to be introduced as in racing with the intention of making every cricketer and subsequently every team *of equal ability*, leading to close and exciting finishes.

Bowlers

Weights would be adjusted weekly depending on the particular bowler's position in the national averages. The leading bowler could carry anything up to three stone extra. Pieces of lead would be inserted into a special back pack, and the bowler would need to be 'weighed in' at the end of each over. If a bowler should still prove superior he would wear boots with no spikes and specially polished soles.

Batsmen

The weighting system was rejected here in favour of specially graded dark glasses – the more successful the batsman, the darker the glasses. The leading batsman would be completely blind-folded with a square made of yellow jersey. It would of course be a great honour to be the current holder of the yellow jersey, more than compensating, it was felt, for the undeniably increased risk of serious injury.

Another suggestion was that the better the batsman, the less protective gear he might be allowed. As the top batsman would then technically be naked, it was felt that some of the current players might actually *gain* from this 'handicap', for the bowlers and fielders might be laughing so much that their ability to play would be seriously impaired.

For the less successful batsman 'Not Out First Ball' could be employed. 'Not Out Second Ball', 'Third Ball', 'Fourth Ball', etc., were also considered to be a useful handicapping system, but it was felt that no one should have a handicap of more than 'Not Out Fiftieth Ball'.

MORE GAMES PER DAY

A minority felt that one game a day was not enough. A suggestion that no games should last longer than fifty minutes and that a new game should be started every hour on the hour was defeated by thirteen votes to six with twenty-three abstaining.

A motion put forward by the representative of a Yorkshire splinter group that the committee's terms of reference should be changed from Brighter Cricket to DULLER Cricket was defeated by a show of hands. The show of one more hand than there were people present was accounted for by an umpire who absentmindedly thought he was signalling a six!

CHAPTER THIRTEEN
CRICKET TACTICS

EVERY captain will inevitably be criticised for his tactics. One method of deflecting some of this criticism is to employ some of the lesser known and consequently surprising tactics. Again I am indebted to my cricketing friends from all over the world for their helpful suggestions. I hope they prove useful to your team.

LONG BOUNDARY

The placing of the boundary rope a considerable distance from the wicket to reduce the number of fours scored by a batsman in any innings. Long boundaries are the responsibility of supporters who should discreetly extend the boundary rope during the course of a match.

NINTH SLIP

The placing of a ninth slip by West Indian captains when bowling against England teams. By curious contrast the habit of a tenth slip and a wicket-keeper, thereby reducing a team to eleven fielders and no fast bowler, is commonly used by England teams.

LONG BOWLING

The bowler starts his run-up beyond the boundary approaching the wicket with a *slow*, drawn-out step. Long bowling when conducted proficiently can reduce the over rate to less than one an hour. In the first slow-bowling international in 1973,

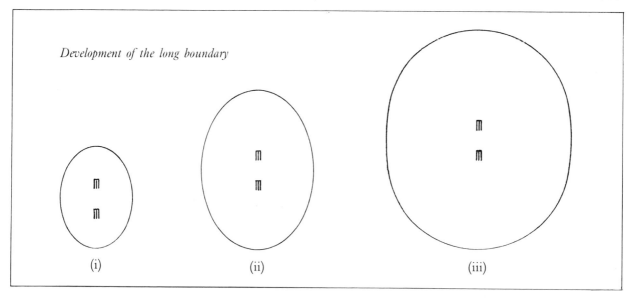

Development of the long boundary

(i)   (ii)   (iii)

the first ball itself took sixty minutes to deliver when the bowler boarded a bus outside the ground and spent the next hour working his way back to the wicket. The ball itself was incidentally called 'no-ball'. Bowling figures for the first five-day international:

PRESIDENT'S XI			
Overs	M	W	R
Cambwell	2	2	0	0
Tipley	1	1	0	0
Griddle	0.5	0.5	0	0
Pomp	0	0	0	0

TOURISTS			
Overs	M	W	R
Stickey	0	0	0	0
Broadbent	0	0	0	0
Troadmore	0	0	0	0
Scrimp	−1	−1	−1	−20

NO WICKET

A useful tactic to avoid an ignominious defeat. *One-no-wicket* is called when one wicket is lost and a team allowed to bat on with two stumps. *Two-no-wicket* is called when two wickets are missing. *Three-no-wicket* is often called when no wickets are available and is often associated with *no-bat, no-kit-bag,* and *no-car-where-you-left-it-half-an-hour-ago.*

SUDDEN BOWLING

Sudden bowling is the name given by bowlers to the art of releasing the ball before you reach the wicket. The act, performed suddenly and without warning, can easily catch unsuspecting batsmen out, the ball being delivered to him several seconds before he expects to receive it.

Try and develop your sudden bowling technique to allow the ball to leave the hand when it is least expected; when one is walking back to one's mark, when the hand is still in the pocket, or when you are apparently redirecting your field and the batsman looks round to see which players

Sudden bowling. Try and develop your sudden bowling technique to allow the ball to leave the hand when it is least expected such as when one is walking back to one's mark

have moved. Sudden bowling when drinks are being taken has been disallowed for several years.

SUDDEN BATTING

Not nearly as successful as sudden bowling, the stroke being played several seconds before the ball is delivered. Batsmen given to sudden batting usually find they have then to endure an embarrassing few seconds in which they struggle to regain their composure and ground before the ball actually arrives. Very popular with village sides, where batsmen may make two or three attempts to hit the ball before it arrives.

SYNCHRONIZED CRICKET

A new development by the 'Brighter Cricket Company'. Captains encourage players to move around the field rather than stay in the same position, in accordance with specially arranged choreography. Teams attempting the technique have reported that, provided the dance steps are well-rehearsed beforehand, there is no reason why bowling figures should in any way suffer, while

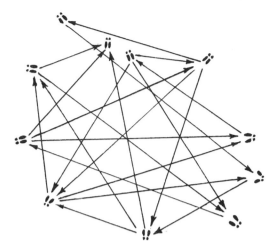

Above: First steps for a simple dance routine for eleven cricketers

Below: Synchronised batting. A new sport for the Olympics?

(3) Roller disco

(4) Smooch (not recommended in Australia)

Wicket

Umpire

Above: Simple steps for an effective routine for fast right-arm bowler

Below: The author executes a near perfect paso doble in front of a full house at Lord's

spectators have expressed themselves pleasantly surprised at how interesting the new technique is to watch.

See also Synchronized Batting, above.

CHOREOGRAPHED BOWLING

The bowler approaches the wicket in one of the following dance-steps:

(1) Disco

(2) Body popping

CATCH JUGGLING

Instead of catching the ball cleanly, the fielder allows the ball to spin from one hand to the other in the following manner:

Practise – try to work up a routine with other players:

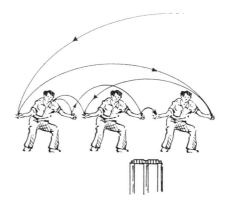

Do be sure fellow-players know the routine before you begin. Many a useful catch has been put down by players attempting *catch juggling* only to realise too late that their fellow-players have not learnt the same routine.

Above left: *Scene from a choreographed cricket match:* Romeo and Juliet and Northamptonshire. *Here Romeo looks for an outside edge off a medium-paced seamer*

Above right: *Romeo shows his full love for Juliet with a pull to leg. The Northamptonshire wicket-keeper appeals (though not to me)*

Far left: *Ballroom cricket. Betty and Ivor Nugent take to the floor from the bandstand end. Viv Richards (not seen) is the batsman. Ivor Nugent is perhaps best known as one of the Bedser triplets*

Left: Side-by-Side-by-Cowdray. *A new musical revue opens to a mixed reception in London*

CHAPTER FOURTEEN

UMPIRES: FRIEND OR FOE?

I<small>T</small> is seldom realised that a team is playing the umpire as much as playing its opponents. *Every care should be taken to defeat the umpire in much the same way as one would attempt to defeat one's opponents.*

INTIMIDATION BY THE BATSMAN

Intimidation is an ugly word to use. But it is accurate. Smerge is another ugly word. The early stages of intimidation can be quite gentle. The odd drive straight down the wicket, narrowly missing the umpire's head on the first bounce, is a fair enough opener. But be sure to mention you have missed him on purpose. A sharply hooked shot in the direction of square leg, causing the umpire to dive frantically for shelter, is a useful follow-up. Do of course be certain to offer profuse apologies for any injury you might have caused but be sure the umpire knows your intention to repeat the shot at the earliest opportunity. This will naturally throw him into a state of nervous tension in which his mind is unlikely to be given to the task in hand.

After these preliminary exchanges, it is acceptable to adopt more subtle approaches. A bat that comes clean out of the grasp and heads for the umpire's neck is a potent way of reminding the umpire of your intentions. Always remember to fix your eyes firmly upon the part of the umpire's anatomy at which you intend to direct your next shot, causing him to lose composure.

BOWLING

When bowling, you should seek psychologically to upset the umpire by asking his advice on small matters of practice or law. Ask if your trailing foot is all right; consult him about the light. Draw him into your confidence. When you come to appeal he will feel he is betraying a good friend if he turns you down and will seek to give you the benefit of any doubtful claim.

Try also to draw the umpire into conversation about the rules of cricket. Secure from him his opinions and views. He will naturally feel part of the game and be grateful for this hand of friendship. When you appeal you will be able to fix him honestly with your eye as you might a trusted friend. He will find it impossible to turn down such an appeal.

PRE-MATCH

If you can gain access to the umpire before the game, take him to one side and tell him openly and honestly that he is to be perfectly impartial. Tell him you will accept nothing but truth and honesty. Drill into him your belief in the integrity of the game. He will think you are a fair and candid sportsman and will naturally treat any appeal you make thereafter with respect and concern. Purely on the basis of probability he will award a reasonable number of appeals. Make fifty polite bogus claims and you are sure to take the ten wickets you need.

OUT STAY OUT ONE SHORT TWO SHORT

BYE BYE BYE NO BALL NO BALL
(but look in pocket
and you'll find one)

WIDE I AM AN AEROPLANE. I USED TO BE A
DRIVING INSTRUCTOR I AM A LITTLE TEAPOT
SHORT & STOUT

Rodney Bankercliffe. The world's most famous umpire demonstrates an experimental version of his new signal for 'leg over the wicket' bowling

Rodney takes the controversial catch that dismissed the last Essex man in the Essex v. Hampshire County Championship match in 1948. Rodney, who took six catches without bowling a ball in the match, was later suspended from the game

IF YOU CANNOT GAIN ACCESS TO THE UMPIRE

If you cannot gain access to the umpire before the game, then a good alternative is to make a quick inspection of the car park and ascertain which car he owns. Arrange for your own team to move their cars in such a way that they surround and block in his vehicle. Explain the situation to the umpire as he is about to take the field, point out that foolishly your players have blocked him in, apologise and ask if he wishes the cars to be moved. He will tell you to think nothing of it; it is of no concern to him after all. He will barely even give the matter a thought.

Early in the innings arrange for one or more of the batsmen not at the wicket to move their cars a fraction closer to the umpire's vehicle. Ensure they do this with sufficient noise to attract the umpire's attention. The umpire on seeing this will naturally become slightly alarmed and lose concentration. Continue this ploy to increase his uncertainty. Should an appeal be made against you, the player at the wheel of the car should rev up his engine as loudly as possible and start easing it nearer the umpire's vehicle. He will at this point lose all interest in the cricket match and turn to see what is happening. By the time he has satisfied himself that his car isn't about to be damaged he will have forgotten what the appeal was for and will have no option but to turn it down. This technique should be used sparingly. Do it too often and the umpire will smell a rat and become all the more vigilant.

OTHER TIPS

Drugs It is not considered fair sport to tamper with an umpire by means of drugs. Quite apart from anything else it is totally uncertain how a drugged official will respond and there is every chance that his decisions will be more severe than ever. Indeed, there is even a chance that he might give the whole team out in one go as is often the case with Indian umpires.

Sexual inducements No. Umpires are asexual and unlikely to respond.

Financial inducements Yes. Specify what the money is for beforehand and get it in writing. It is no use complaining afterwards if a certain expensive decision is not made.

CHAPTER FIFTEEN

CRICKETOBILIA

WHO knows what priceless pieces of cricketobilia you may find lying around your attic? Nothing quite as rare as W.G.'s missing left spat, or as exotic as the Nawab of Pataudi's elephant, perhaps. But any cricket lover will understand the thrill of finding a dust-covered first edition of Shillinglaw's *Some More Great Welsh Long Stops* as I did recently in a Norfolk rectory. The following are just a few of the wonderful souvenirs sent so generously to me for my charity auction in aid of The Distressed Friends Of Northamptonshire Cricket.

F.T. BUSBY'S CHEWING GUM

F.T. Busby made many memorable catches while in the field for his club, holding many chances that seemed impossible. Only after he retired did he reveal his technique, for crouching down in the field, he would insert a mouthful of chewing gum, removing it as the ball was delivered and allowing it to form a sticky mass in his hand. By this method, Busby was able to 'hold' virtually anything that so much as touched his palm, the only difficulty arising when he was expected to make a quick throw to the wicket, an action he (needless to say) found totally impossible, having instead to sprint to the wicket as fast as he could with the ball still stuck to his hand.

F.C. SIMMONS' RUBBER WICKETS

Simmons was an inventor rather than a cricketer and after visiting a match one day he concluded that a considerable amount of time and effort could be saved if the wickets and bails did not need to be reset and assembled after every dismissal. He therefore set about designing a set of all-rubber wickets which would immediately right themselves to an erect position if struck, a bell ringing to announce that a contact had been made.

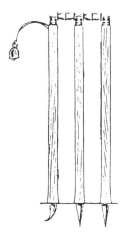

Unfortunately the wickets proved disastrous in experimental tests, the rubber used being far too rigid for the task required. Instead of collapsing then re-erecting, they simply absorbed the force of the ball and flung it back at the bowler with all the velocity with which it had arrived; a sharp ring from the bell adding to the panic thus caused.

J. H. Lancing's bat

J.H. LANCING'S BAT

This is the bat that Lancing used when scoring his memorable 2451 not out against himself while playing for the schizophrenic wing of his local long-stay mental home. Lancing's achievement of scoring so many runs off his own bowling led the schizophrenic team to score a truly remarkable total of 14,971 runs, the match being played against themselves.

J.II. LANCING'S BALL

This is the ball that Lancing used when taking ten wickets for no runs in both innings during the return fixture.

R.M.B. BROWNWOLDS' LAST PENCIL

R.M.B. Brownwolds was perhaps the greatest cricket scorer that ever lived. His feats with the pencil and rubber were legendary and he would regularly attract capacity crowds to the matches in which he was scorer, all eager to watch the great man meticulously record the score. His final pencil, left as it was when he had finished with it,

completely unsharpened, is a testament to perhaps the greatest scorekeeper this country has seen.

SIR BENJAMIN WIPPLE'S SILVER TEA SERVICE

This is the same service from which Sir Benjamin insisted his tea be served during every tea interval of games in which he played. Indeed, while other, more humble players, made do with the normal china cups, Sir Benjamin struck a distinguished figure as he took his tea alone, served from the silver service by his faithful servant Manstable.

R. M. B. Brownwolds' last pencil

The cut and style of this elegant dandy must have contributed greatly to his success with the bat; opposing bowlers being unwilling to offer true challenges to a man of such dashing dignity and poise.

C.R. CRAVEN-BARCLAY'S CRICKET BOOTS

Craven-Barclay was a fierce left-arm quick bowler who during the period 1880 to 1890 dismissed a remarkable number of batsmen with his cunningly deceptive deliveries that appeared to travel in a quite unique manner. The absence of time-lapse or slow-motion photography at the time prevented a close analysis of what we now know to be the case, which was that Craven-Barclay had developed a sleight of hand and foot that was invisible to even the keenest of eyes, for he would allow his bowling arm to meet his foot just as the ball was released from his hand, the ball propelled forward not only by the normal motion of his hand but also by the drop kick that thus ensued. The result, performed at speed, was devastating in its speed and accuracy. Later examination of Craven-Barclay's boots using modern cricket forensic techniques revealed the clearly-indented spot where regular contact with the ball had worn a mark.

C. R. Craven-Barclay's left cricket boot

Below: The Craven-Barclay boot in action

BAMBER DICKINS' GLOVES

Known as 'nimble fingers' for his sharp and alert speed behind the stumps, Bamber was county and country wicket-keeper for many years, his safe and dependable hands always a welcome addition to any side. After he retired from the game, he left his gloves to his local club who had them framed and mounted on the wall. Legend has it that young wicket-keepers wishing to emulate Bamber's achievements should insert their hands in the gloves for five minutes before going out to play to draw extra dexterity from the old man's ghostly fingers. Each year the insides of the gloves were scraped clean with a tooth pick and the contents mixed together to form a rare and much valued deodorant for men: 'Old Stumps'.

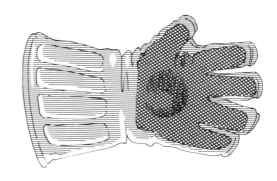

ANGUS KART'S CAP

Constructed of solid pine with a brass accoutrement, this surely must have been the first example of protective clothing used by a cricketer. The cap, made from turned pine, was an ideal safeguard, being both sturdy and hard. However in

wet weather when the wood became moist, the cap would expand, only to contract again as it dried, clasping the head firmly and painfully, no effort to remove it being successful. Kart himself (known in his younger days as 'Orson') was often left with the task of walking home at night, the wooden cap still firmly stuck to his head, an experience that contributed to his early retirement from the game, the constant headaches and flashing lights proving too much to bear.

OWZAT!

Another rare item that came into my possession was a collector's set of *Owzat!* Many of you will be familiar with the game, but how many have seen a set as complete as the one below? Few schoolboys can have passed through life without once playing the game of *Owzat!* Its simple formula has passed the test of time. But as with all good ideas, a thousand more less-than-good are spawned – these are the ones that didn't catch on – that never made it into the schoolboy's pocket. To assemble the genuine article, simply fold along the dotted line and glue:

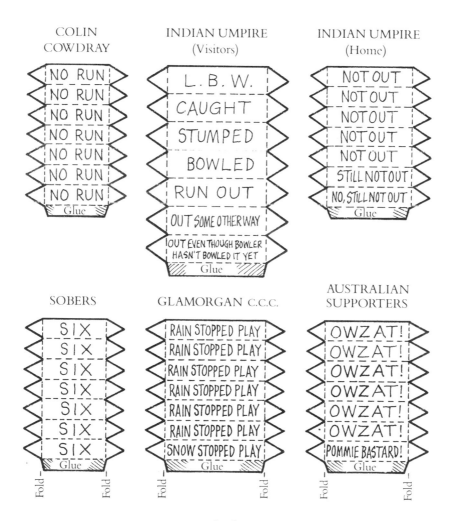

'Geoffrey Boycott' – a delightful game which is already a collector's item. Made entirely from wood, just like the real thing. Offers hours of enjoyment for all the family – unlike the real thing

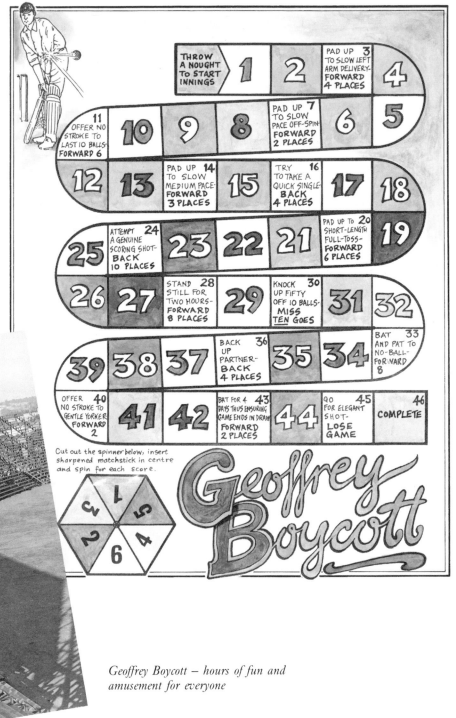

THROW A NOUGHT TO START INNINGS
1
2
PAD UP 3 TO SLOW LEFT ARM DELIVERY- FORWARD 4 PLACES
4
11 OFFER NO STROKE TO LAST 10 BALLS- FORWARD 6
10
9
8
PAD UP 7 TO SLOW PACE OFF-SPIN- FORWARD 2 PLACES
6
5
12
13
PAD UP 14 TO SLOW MEDIUM PACE- FORWARD 3 PLACES
15
TRY 16 TO TAKE A QUICK SINGLE- BACK 4 PLACES
17
18
ATTEMPT 24 A GENUINE SCORING SHOT- BACK 10 PLACES
25
23
22
21
PAD UP TO 20 SHORT-LENGTH FULL-TOSS- FORWARD 6 PLACES
19
26
27
STAND 28 STILL FOR TWO HOURS- FORWARD 8 PLACES
29
KNOCK 30 UP FIFTY OFF 10 BALLS- MISS TEN GOES
31
32
39
38
37
BACK 36 UP PARTNER- BACK 4 PLACES
35
34
BAT 33 AND PAT TO NO-BALL- FORWARD 8
OFFER 40 NO STROKE TO GENTLE YORKER- FORWARD 2
41
42
BAT FOR 4 43 DAYS THUS ENSURING GAME ENDS IN DRAW FORWARD 2 PLACES
44
GO 45 FOR ELEGANT SHOT- LOSE GAME
46 COMPLETE

Cut out the spinner below, insert sharpened matchstick in centre and spin for each score.

3 1 5 2 6 4

Geoffrey Boycott

Geoffrey Boycott – hours of fun and amusement for everyone

CHAPTER SIXTEEN

ETIQUETTE TO AND FROM THE PAVILION

NOWADAYS too little attention is given to what is probably the most important part of the batsman's game – the Long Walk to and from the pavilion. These walks can be sobering journeys. Outward to the crease the batsman knows fear, trepidation, suspicion. Inward to the pavilion perhaps he anticipates a chilling reception from a hostile crowd.

I myself on one occasion fell down the pavilion steps at Lord's having, out of sheer nervousness, tied both my bootlaces together. It was the St John's Ambulance man, after he had set my leg, who first drew my attention to Peter Risedale-Forest's *The Gentleman's Game* with its excellent chapter on just this subject. I am grateful to St Bastion Press for allowing me to reprint extracts from Risedale-Forest's work which is now sadly out of print.

Left: *The author demonstrates a textbook upright stance as he returns to the pavilion*
Right: *The author demonstrates a loutish, casual return to the pavilion (fielder).*
He is accompanied by some lesser players

ETIQUETTE – 'TO AND FROM THE CREASE'

Before Leaving the Pavilion

Before leaving the pavilion, check you have with you all you require. Check particularly that you are carrying a bat. (E.S. Turner of Minor Counties East actually reached the crease and faced three balls before he realised he had taken to the field without his bat.)

E. S. Turner

While inside the pavilion check to make sure you have on a sufficient weight of clothing. A cursory glance at the weather should be sufficient but in the case of doubt follow the climate chart below to provide an easy reference to suitability:

5°C	3 jumpers, 2 shirts, vest
10°C	2 jumpers, 2 shirts, vest
15°C	2 jumpers, 1 shirt, vest
20°C	2 jumpers, 1 shirt
25°C	1 jumper, 1 shirt
30°C	1 shirt
35°C	*Nude*

Remember it may be difficult or impossible to change your attire once at the crease, so always try to prepare well in advance for the considered clime.

From Pavilion to Crease

It is here that most batsmen make their mark on a match, and *not at the crease itself!* A fine or distinctive walk can mark a man out for selection or applause even before he has faced a ball. T.M. Elliot (Gloucestershire, 1928–37) regularly drew applause for his walk to the crease. M.F. Banyard became a firm fixture in the Kent side from 1907 to 1913 though he did not score a single run, simply on account of his magnificent and impressive gait to, and almost immediately from, the wicket.

The choice of route is important too. While it is in order to prolong or delay your arrival at the crease by a modicum of divergence, care should be exercised lest the habit becomes too extreme or prolonged. A vital extra few seconds to control one's nerves and irritate one's opponents, or even to delay what might seem an inevitable defeat, is perfectly respectable. Examples of successful walks that may be usefully copied are shown on page 62.

Examples of unacceptable entries are shown on page 63.

To further enhance your prestige and standing while walking to the wicket it is also quite in order to execute the following series of advancements:

Shoes Tying and untying shoes on the long walk to the crease is an extremely acceptable pursuit. Take care not to tie or untie any one shoe more than is reasonably acceptable: two or three times is normally sufficient. You should not usually take further pairs out to the crease with you to untie along the way. Always make an elaborate gesture when tying and untying shoes. Stop, bend down, and make a

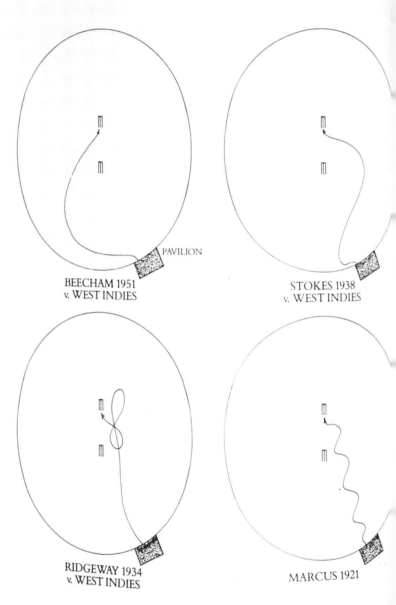

BEECHAM 1951
v. WEST INDIES

PAVILION

STOKES 1938
v. WEST INDIES

RIDGEWAY 1934
v. WEST INDIES

MARCUS 1921

Acceptable walks

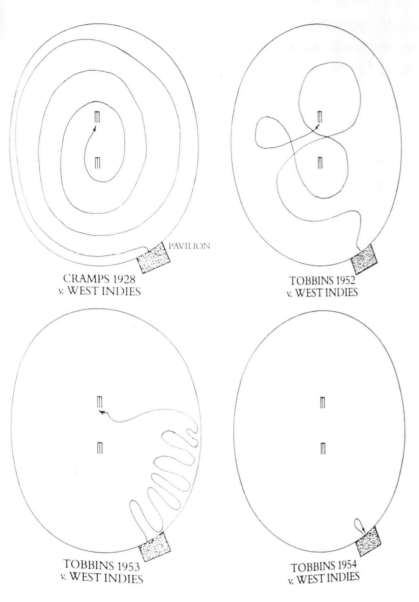

CRAMPS 1928
v. WEST INDIES

PAVILION

TOBBINS 1952
v. WEST INDIES

TOBBINS 1953
v. WEST INDIES

TOBBINS 1954
v. WEST INDIES

Unacceptable walks

florid and extravagant show with the hand before doing up the lace.

WARNING On no account attempt to tie or untie laces when actually walking. Not only can the effect be quite unbecoming but you may find in your haste that you are tying your shoes to each other*.

Bat Finger your bat with care and pride as you make for the crease. It always pays dividends if a batsman treats his bat with love and affection.

Gloves The same remark might apply to the gloves, which should be put on as one makes for the crease. This conveys the air of a man about to take part in a serious or businesslike act.

Other Useful Tips Do not allow the legs to wobble conspicuously. If necessary affix a small, discreet bamboo cane to those moving parts which might tremble. Do not allow your head to *sink below* shoulder level. Do not grin or wave to fielders or acknowledge their presence in any other way than by a scornful glance. Do not spit, foul, or abuse the turf. Do not, when asked for one's guard, reply, 'It's all right, I won't be here for long'.

*See the introduction to this chapter.

Quite clearly the demands of etiquette change with the level of the game. Whilst the aforementioned may be of valuable assistance for the professional, a useful alternative for the novice player is Potter's *A Day In the Field*, a chronological account of suitable behaviour throughout the day for the village cricketer, published herewith as in Potter's original text.

The diary of a village cricketer

7.50	Wake up.
7.55	Select clean sock (white).
7.58	Select second nearly clean sock (off-white).
8.15	Scrape last year's mould from cricket boot.
8.17	Try to stick sole of cricket boot back in place with an empty tube of glue.
8.26	Discover large hole in rear of cricket trousers. Repair with empty tube of glue. Try trousers on. Attempt to unstick trousers from underpants.
10.03	Arrive at ground. Discover hole in path. Remove bike from large hole. Pick self up.
10.21	Inspect wicket.
10.31	Attempt to remove large molehill from centre of crease.
10.32	Discover why spade had 'do not use' sticker on handle.
10.33	Try to stick shovel handle and blade back together – search for bandage for ankle.
10.34	Move sightscreen.
10.37	Clean up remains of sightscreen. Check for full extent of woodworm elsewhere.
11.40	Inspect kit bag. Remove slug from inside jock-strap. Repack one pad with rolled-up newspaper. Straighten cricket bat by banging against side of pavilion. Make mental note to explain to rest of team how one side of pavilion came to be missing.
12.31	Lunch with rest of team.
12.58	More lunch with rest of team.
1.08	Lunch with visitors.
1.43	More lunch with visitors.
1.52	Feel bones filling up with confidence – visit toilet to empty confidence.
2.03	Toss up. Visitors to bat.
2.04	Asked to field in deep.

2.06	Spot cowpat in outfield.
2.07	Chase cover drive. Miss ball, find cowpat.
2.23	Batsman attempts difficult hook shot. Bat comes free from his hand. Dive for cover as bat hurtles in my direction. Luckily manage to avoid bat. Unluckily don't manage to avoid cowpat.
2.56	Brought on to bowl:

First ball clears batsman's head by three feet.

Second ball clears second slip's head by three feet.

Third ball reaches batsman on third bounce, batsman misses, ball stops dead before reaching stumps.

Fourth ball – forget to let go of ball. Discover ball in own hand, appeal for a catch.

Fifth ball – remember to let go. Ball leaves hand, braces leave trousers. Trousers fall down, braces spring up. Braces wrap themselves around neck.

Sixth ball – hits batsman on kneecaps. Batsman retires injured.

4.02	Make dramatic attempt at diving catch. Catch ball, see cowpat, drop ball, avoid cowpat. Ball falls into cowpat. Batsmen run six while searching for a stick with which to poke ball free.
4.15	Tea interval – during meal become aware of a sudden large swelling to groin. Ask captain – a registered doctor – for a second opinion. Discover have been sitting on cricket ball. Much relieved and finish tea in comfort. Discover ball to be slightly squashed as a result. Decide to say nothing of it and hope other team do not notice.
5.18	Pad up ready to bat. Great difficulty in finding pads. Strap seems to have been put on the wrong way round. Discover too late that pads are on inside out.
5.20	Insert guard – immediately experience sudden burning sensation to loins – remove guard, upset to find fellow players have been using it as an ashtray. Remove remaining stubs from trousers with difficulty.

5.34	At last called upon to bat. Surprised how big the stumps appear to be this year. Use bat to remove three-inch divot from batting crease. Twist shoulder as a result. Spend five minutes back in changing room rubbing liniment into injury, return to crease, take guard, take a few practice strokes in preparation – knock entire row of stumps down flat. Wait for stumps to be reassembled.
5.36	'Play' called. Make forward defensive shot to first ball. Miss ball by some three feet. Call for fellow batsman to take a quick single. Scramble back to wicket as he fails to back up. Not pleased by his explanation that the ball was already in the wicket-keeper's gloves before run even started. Point out 'Opportunism is a major element of my game'.
5.37	Offer no shot to next delivery. Hit on chest. Have difficulty regaining breath getting up off ground.
5.38	Attempt to hook an off-spinner. Inwardly rather pleased at the precision with which the cleverly placed shot passes clean through the slip fielder's legs. Run two.
5.39	Miss next two deliveries completely. Make big show of the fact that I knew exactly what I was doing. Confidence now beginning to flow within.
5.40	Clean bowled off next ball. Trust me to have to face the most difficult ball of the afternoon. On my way back to the pavilion feel sure I felt a drop of rain fall.
5.42	Rain now falling steadily. Admire courage of players in continuing to play through it.
5.49	Game abandoned when lightning strikes scoreboard for the third time in five minutes.
5.59–11.00	Refreshment.
11.38	Attempt to discover where own house has been left.

CHAPTER SEVENTEEN

SOME OTHER ASHES

(Gloucester)

(Northampton)

Laid to rest in July 1937 on the actual ground where he had been a faithful follower since boyhood. The unusual feature of his departure was not the position or manner, nor even the timing, but that he insisted on a headstone being erected on the grave, a request which no one, bearing in mind the tragic circumstances of his death (and indeed that of the hamster as well) felt able to deny. A four-foot cross was therefore set up on the pitch at silly point, an edifice that caused no end of batting problems as a ball driven smartly square would rear back at the poor batsman with all the speed with which it was dispatched. At the end of the season sentiment gave way to common sense, and also to safety, for no less than eight batsmen received concussion from the rebounds and the grave was discreetly moved from the crease to behind the groundsman's hut.

Denzil was the first supporter to be buried while a match was actually in progress, this being his one last wish. He had specifically requested that the match should not stop for the ceremony and so it was that on the afternoon of 15 June 1952 his cortège skirted the perimeter of the pitch, the match between Gloucestershire and Northamptonshire being at a delicate state of play. Had that been the only notable feature of this departure it would still have been an historic event, but more memorable still was the moment when the bearers laid the open coffin on the edge of the boundary for a few seconds, just as a massive hit was made from the visiting Gloucestershire skipper. The ball landed in the coffin, lodging perfectly in Denzil's stiffened hand, and as the hand was inside the boundary at that moment and the ball had not touched the ground, the catch was adjudged to have been made. Perhaps the most remarkable dismissal of all time, and certainly the highlight of Donnavan's life. Or rather death.

(*Lancashire*)

Buried 1948. Lifelong Lancashire supporter, insisted he be buried on the Old Trafford ground he loved so dearly. His ghost is now believed to live on the ground and on chilly autumn evenings after the season has closed, his ghost has been seen moving swiftly up and down the wicket making the century that eluded him all his life.

(*Somerset*)

Buried 1911. For many years his urn lay undisturbed on a shelf in the committee room, but following one disastrously wet summer during which the pitch cut up badly, the controversial decision was taken to spread the ashes on the wicket to help the bowlers gain a foothold. The ruse worked delightfully and many still believe Coppiethorne was responsible for the county pulling off the Championship that season.

(*Leicester*)

A tragic death in 1939 in the arms of his eighteen-year-old mistress when he was barely ninety-eight years old took this colourful character away from the club he had supported for the best part of sixty years. His one wish was to be buried on the pitch like Stickley of Gloucester but the groundsman at the time steadfastly refused, pointing out quite rightly the grave damage a burial would make to the wicket. Eventually a compromise was reached. The boundary rope would be extended by a matter of a few feet at its furthest point to take in the extra land required for a grave. This way it would be possible for Grosvenor to be buried on the pitch without the ground suffering noticeable impairment. This compromise, now sadly no more, was for many years known as Grosvenor's snitch, the extra few feet allowing alert fielders to make more than one unexpected catch.

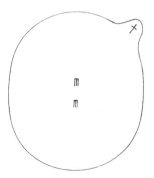

Grosvenor's snitch

(Warwick)

Spot had visited the ground with his master for many seasons and it came as a tragic loss when he escaped his leash during the tea interval in a match against Essex on 8 August 1958 and ran on to the pitch to be fatally run over by the heavy roller. It was a sad and poignant end for a dog which had spent so much time at the ground to be finally rolled to rest in such a fateful way, and as a tribute to him the committee agreed to his owner's wish that he be buried on the ground.

The ashes were spread the following Saturday, and as a mark of respect, the same roller which had killed him was used to roll the ashes into the ground. Since that day the spot where Spot died has been known as 'Spot's Spot' and whenever the roller is used over that stretch of ground, the groundsman always removes his hat as a mark of respect.

CHAPTER EIGHTEEN

A SHORT HISTORY OF LADIES' CRICKET

THERE are many who still think of ladies' cricket as a contradiction in terms. I disagree, but only for a very short chapter. The first game of ladies' cricket took place in June 1906, when the Lady Walkingholme-Slowly invited a party of female friends home for tea. Refreshments being finished, the women became engaged in the topic of emancipation and the suffragette movement, and a hot dispute arose during which the question of whether women might be able to compete equally with men was raised. To prove the matter, the more liberal women present took it upon themselves to arrange a game of cricket, whereupon the issue could be decided once and for all. This first ladies' cricket match was brought swiftly to a close by the local constabulary who, seeing the game, believed an affray to be taking place and arrested the seventeen women involved.

The first ladies' international took place on 11 May 1926 between England and Italy. The Italian women proved no match for the Englishwomen. During the match the Italians, unused to the new game, ran around the edge of the pitch as in a rounders match and were easily dismissed.

During the 1937 Test between England and Australia, the controversial 'bodyline' crisis that had arisen in the male game some years earlier flared up in the women's in a slightly different form, the English team complaining that the Australians' bodylines were unbecomingly fat and not at all suited to the promotion of the feminine game.

SEVERAL FAMOUS FEMALE PLAYERS

Angela Winco-Ward

Played for England thirteen times. Once beat a man up for calling her unfeminine. Was engaged to the Lord Rather-Loosley who broke off the engagement when he found his fiancée out on the lawns sparring with the local gamekeeper. The Lady Winco-Ward, as well as being a proficient and exciting cricketer, was also an excellent southpaw, boxing many times for England and once travelling to America where she went three rounds with the American Light Heavyweight Champion before he caught her on the ropes.

Babs Barrowclough

Babs was described as the first lady of British cricket. She attended the wicket with flowers and a posy, and was chaperoned wherever she went by a maid who would run down the wicket alongside her holding her bat and embroidery frame. Babs introduced the quilted wicket cover to the English game, an artefact she considered necessary for decency and propriety. She also designed and manufactured the embroidered ball cover which she insisted always be used between overs.

Penelope Winkle

The first lady cricketer to develop and encourage the feminine wicket-keeping position – not with the legs splayed open as in the male game – but in a dignified side-saddle position with the knees clasped firmly together at the side. Penelope was

Babs Barrowclough

Roedean take on Benenden. Roedean won the match on this occasion because it was their turn

The Lady Parkhurst-Parkhurst and Miss Cynthia Snoad take to the pitch in the annual Townswomen's Guild X1 v. MCC 1954. The match was drawn

rude Holroyd, described by many who didn't see her play as the utive darling of British cricket. She also made a proficient first, second and third slip fielder (all at the same time)

Five-stump barefoot cricket. Very popular with cricket wicket manufacturers. Not so popular with shoe manufacturers. Notice the strange flared trousers which allow pads to be worn inside the trouser leg

also instrumental in developing the more feminine cry of 'I wonder if you thought that might possibly be out?' rather than the more masculine shout of 'Owzat!' Penelope took many a graceful catch, standing to her full height as the ball crossed the stumps and taking the ball with all the poise of a ballerina.

Candice Heatman

The 'pretty girl' darling of English cricket in the 1950s. Petite, diminutive, fashionable and strikingly good-looking, she left a career in modelling

Candice Heatman

for cricket. Many of her shots, and certainly her fielding, have been criticised as frivolous and unashamedly exhibitionist. Even picking a ball from the ground she would take the maximum possible opportunity to expose her legs and thighs, pouting lusciously at the men in the crowd.

In pursuit of a ball she would walk unhurriedly rather than run, pause upon reaching it, smile, flutter her eyelids, and wiggle her hips before gently tossing the ball back to the wicket. Against this, it has to be said that she attracted enormous crowds to the games in which she played, and indeed on several occasions the matches actually out-drew the equivalent fixture in the male calendar. She left the game after two seasons to return to modelling, her fees and image having suffered no harm from the publicity.

Cynthia Grooms

Cynthia dominated women's cricket in the early 1960s, introducing many of the changes we see today – butch hairstyles, butch legs, butch arms, and a complete absence of breasts. Cynthia believed that women should compete equally with men or not at all, and spent no little time attending trials with all the major counties trying gamely to play with the boys. It was Cynthia who first encouraged fast bowling in women's cricket and it was her idea to introduce a beer tent at all women's fixtures. She eventually fell foul of the authorities following the controversial 'jock-strap incident' in which she appeared for one match wearing a protector on her head. She never returned to the game after the publicity and was last heard of working on a North Sea oil rig.

CHAPTER NINETEEN
SCHOOLS' CRICKET

THE cradle of English Test sides has always been the public schools, and the victorious side of 1985 contained an unusually large number of players nursed in these privileged establishments. The reports of the 1985 season should therefore give us some pointers to the make-up of our national side in the 1990s.

The account of the Merchant Cobblers XI has been omitted on legal grounds. We are advised that the widely publicised incident concerning the first team and the school chaplain is still *sub judice*.

ST CRISPIN ALLEYNES

Won only one of their last forty matches. C.J. Goodbent was rusticated for events following the junior house match in which Cosgrove received an entire cricket bat down his throat. Drew with the MCC, Merchant Bagley's and Frombley High. Lost to the RAF and Russia.

ST RECTUM'S

Began the season disastrously when they played themselves and lost. Beat King Thresher's, Bingles and Latimer Beaumont. R. Lock and Letterley were the spearhead bowlers and R.D. Bailey had an exciting season in the showers.

The Under Fourteens lived up to their name and were frequently out for under fourteen.

UPPINGCREEK
(removed)

Gained splendid victories over Lincolnshire, Womble, King's RGS and China (away). Hinkley and Mucktrodert achieved creditable success with the bat, and Robinson with the sightscreen. Woolsacks were not awarded this year.

CLIFTON-DOWNSIDE

Barston was captain. Challingford (seven not out) and Bidhurst (twelve not in) were among the more successful players. Romboid had a good season behind the stumps, till Cranhurst spotted him and told him to stop hiding and go to his lessons.

BEACHCROFT UPPER

Beat Bradfield and St Edmund's but lost to Oundle, Bedford and Radley Superior. J.F. Connington and D. Cobham had to be treated for minor burns after an exciting finish to the parents' match, and Housegood-Marks had to have a slight incision to his right ventral cavity repaired when the school doctor performed a partial appendectomy on him by mistake during the Junior Sixth Cup Match.

BEAUWOOD UPPER

Their captain, Sheridan, achieved success with the bat and ball, learning which was which at last. Wainwright proved a useful wicket-keeper, keeping the wickets for the entire term in his locker before anyone realised what was happening. Connington and Denvill were sent down following an incident in the changing-room after the Combined Services Match.

ST WILLINGBOROUGH MIDDLE SCHOOL

Inconsistent batting and lack of attacking penetration, together with a serious outbreak of dysentery, reduced the team's strength considerably. Cholera broke out during the match with Beddingdown Inner and scurvy was discovered in the school jock-strap after the end of term masonics.

REPTILE LATTERDAY
(*Mixed*)

Scrippage and Dongle were the school's most useful fielders, taking a brace of catches each in the match with Limpopo Girls. Scrotcher received his colours following a particularly exciting attempt to score with Miss Plumstead, who left the school hurriedly afterwards.

HAILEYBUCKS AND OAT

Yomps and Tipples were punishing batsmen, and Whittaker and Congleton as (in-swing) batsmen took no time at all to assert themselves in Big Hall. Crippin took wickets regularly, but was made to bring them back. A disappointment was the failure of M.A. Fairbairn – the captain – to reproduce his figures of last season when he broke into the scoreboard hut but couldn't find a pencil and rubber with which to do the alterations.

DELFONT MIDDLE

Clipping did extremely well, as did Bombodiddle Minor. School won ten matches and drew another after an exciting fight took place between the boys and the visitors from St Benelux. Regular scuffles took place with many other schools. Captain H.N. Chapman did well to punch at least six visiting captains soundly in the face and R.H.M. Food capped another good season by killing a spectator in the MCC match.

DENISTORM RGS

A. Hitler had a sparkling term taking no less than 800 wickets without the loss of a single tank. Ottley and Galtieri were useful with the bat. Frome-Wilson and Lattley successfully broke wind in the changing-room on eight occasions – a school record.

MERCHANT TAYLORS, BETHNAL GREEN

Cohen, Cohen and Cohen made useful innings and Goldenstein, Rosencratz and Hymie Bernsteinberger took two for three in three balls, or to you, one for three in two balls. The scorebook has not yet been approved by the school's accountants.

CHAPTER TWENTY

ANOTHER BOOK OF RECORDS

For several years I have made a point of collecting interesting or unusual records. An approach to Guinness for inclusion in their volume was met with cursory disinterest. Firmly convinced that the facts amassed deserve a wider audience, I take the opportunity to include them in this volume, confident that your judgment will prove me right . . . anyway it's nasty bitter stuff, isn't it, Guinness . . . well, I think so!

THE LONGEST CRY OF 'OWZAT!'
Took place in a match between Perth and N.W. Queensland in 1938. Terry Yakkawalla appealed for an lbw decision and was still to be heard wailing ten hours later.

THE MOST RUNS SCORED IN A SEASON BY AN UMPIRE
Thomas Cardigan (the galloping umpire) achieved this feat during the 1896 season when he amassed no less than 2471 runs by sprinting up and down the wicket alongside the batsmen, ignoring the players' appeals to him to stop fooling around.

THE GREATEST NUMBER OF BALLS SENT DOWN IN ONE DELIVERY
The record goes to Jeffrey Swindlethorpe, the York bowler who succeeded in delivering no less than thirteen balls down the wicket in one delivery – an achievement that has still to be bettered to this day.

THE MOST WICKET-KEEPERS IN ONE SIDE
The greatest number of wicket-keepers in any one side is eleven, achieved by the Bradford League side, Cumbudleigh, in 1957 when all the players turned out in wicket-keeper's kit. They lost the match by 671 runs, but there were no byes.

THE MOST FAMOUS BATSMAN CALLED DONALD BRADMAN
The most famous batsman called Donald Bradman was the Australian batsman Donald Bradman, who was called Donald Bradman for much of his cricketing life. He later changed his name by deed poll to Sir Donald Bradman.

THE SLOWEST BOWLING EVER
The slowest bowling ever occurred in New Zealand in 1921 when a visiting bowler fell down an exposed manhole as he prepared to run up to the crease. With police and rescue workers it took a total of fourteen hours to release the man, who had become trapped in a drain. Remarkably, he was found to be unhurt and delivered the first ball of his over fourteen hours eleven minutes and twenty-three seconds after he had started his run-up.

THE FASTEST COMPLAINT
The fastest complaint on record occurred in a Welsh league game in August 1969 when the entire Llanfysud team appealed for a wicket before the ball had even been delivered. The complaints that occurred when the umpire dismissed the appeal thus took place before the ball had actually been bowled, making them the fastest complaints that have ever been heard. In an unofficial match, South African team Traansvoorthog appealed for the death sentence

for a batsman in the opponent's side who refused to leave the crease two days before the match in which he was taking part actually began. The appeal was dismissed after the player (coloured) had spent five years in prison awaiting trial.

GREATEST NUMBER OF PADS ON ONE LEG

The greatest number of pads on any one leg was achieved by an Australian player, Garth M. Wonka, who managed to fix eighteen to his leg for a match in July 1947. The pads made it impossible for him to stand properly and on the first ball he toppled over, hit his wicket and was given out.

THE MOST RIDICULOUS REMARK MADE BY AN OPENING BATSMAN

The most ridiculous remark by a player in a first-class match was made during the game between Stalybridge and Todmorden, when the opening batsman on the Todmorden side approached the crease and said, 'I think I'll go for a walk to Plumpkin land.' The batsman, who had been struck on the head by a ball in the previous week's game, went on to score ninety-six not out, sixteen of the runs scored with his head.

THE SMALLEST NUMBER OF PEOPLE INVOLVED IN A FIRST-CLASS GAME OF CRICKET

The smallest number of people involved in a first-class game occurred when Tasmania played North-East Queensland in the All-Australian Trophy. The Tasmania team took the wrong turning and never arrived at the ground, and the North-East Queensland team had a cross-eyed coach driver and didn't arrive till four weeks later. In the event, two Tasmanian batsmen who had made their way to the ground separately, arrived to claim the match for their side and set up the record of two as the smallest number of people ever involved in a first-class game.

THE MOST SENSUAL UMPIRING DECISION

The most sensual umpiring decision was made by the Swedish umpire Sven Allcøcksen in a first-class county match between Middlesex and Essex in which the umpire gave what has been described as the most erotic not-out signal yet seen on a cricket ground. Sensual umpiring, together with the Naturist movement in cricket, have not seen great support and the umpire Allcøcksen himself left the game to join the priesthood shortly after the incident.

THE FASTEST ROLLING OF A PITCH

The fastest rolling took place on 9 May 1964 when, aided by a rocket-powered works dragster, groundsman Bill Bosser of the Perth Amboy Club, Australia, succeeded in rolling a patch of ground ten feet wide and 150 yards long in under two seconds. On the second attempt, the dragster broke free of the roller and destroyed several acres of farmland outside the ground. Groundsman Bosser escaped unhurt. The fastest attempt by a Briton remains the record of four hours thirty-six minutes to roll a patch eighteen yards by ten yards, by groundsman Didcott at Leeds in 1936. The record included two half-hour tea breaks and a twenty-minute break to fill his pipe.

Bill Bosser with his rocket-powered works dragster

THE LEAST SUCCESSFUL ATTEMPT TO MAKE A CATCH

Gerry Fitzgibbon, fielding in the deep in a club match in Sydney, Australia, attempted to make a catch nearly eighty yards away. His brave dive, in the wrong direction and four seconds too late, followed a strenuous tea interval in which he had consumed some eleven pints of lager beer.

THE LONGEST PERIOD WITHOUT MOVING FOR A BATSMAN

There have been several excellent attempts by batsmen to set a new record for standing at the crease without moving. Most occurred in the 1950s, when many first-class players would go for long periods without raising a hand or bat. The record is generally given to Warwickshire batsman Kelvin Murchkeen, who lasted a period of six hours forty-seven minutes at the crease without so much as moving an eyelid. In the period he amassed a creditable score of thirty-seven from leg byes and extras. In a close match at Hove, the Sussex pair Glengrove and Tweedy set up a remarkable stand of five hours eleven minutes during which neither of them moved.

THE MOST RUNS SCORED AT A CRICKET MATCH BY SOMEONE WHO WASN'T THERE

Many examples of runs being scored by cricketers who weren't actually at the ground exist, but without doubt the most spectacular event of this kind took place during the President's Match between the President's team and the local village in Stroud in 1904. The President having been called away on urgent business as soon as he got to the wicket, the opposing team felt it impolite to dismiss the man if he wasn't there and continued to bowl away from his stumps till he returned some three hours later. The result was a succession of disastrous wides that ran the score along nicely. When the President returned to the crease, his business completed, he was pleasantly surprised to find that in his absence his side had notched up a fine seventy-two runs.

GREATEST NUMBER OF PENCILS BROKEN DURING AN INNINGS

A number of records and achievements relate solely to cricket scorers. This one, for the greatest number of pencils broken (unintentionally), is keenly contested by scorers up and down the country. The Kent scorer Arthur Pritchley, in a devastating spell in the Crown Cup on 9 July 1922, achieved a superb ninety-six tips broken in less than three hours. Those who saw the breakages commented on Pritchley's alertness of mind and quickness of hand in keeping the score registered with one hand while operating his pencil sharpener full time with the other. At the end of the period the floor was covered ankle deep in pencil shavings and the result of the game was lost in celebration of Pritchley's achievement. Other noteworthy attempts have been the succession of forty-five, sixty-one, eighty-two, forty-three, thirty-two and seventy-six breakages achieved by the Northamptonshire scorer in a period of six successive matches.*

THE GREAT IVOR PLUNKTON'S FINGERS
Ivor – known as the most daring and courageous of scorers. Here we see the result of many a courageous 'score' behind the pencil – fingers twisted and bent from years of picking up small and shapeless rubbers

BIGGEST RUBBER EVER USED BY A SCORER

The biggest pencil rubber ever used by a scorer was that employed by the Minor Counties East scorer C.W.S. Didcott, whose instrument was

*A competing record for ink nibs bent during a Test was secured by Angus MacDiggle, the famous Scottish scorer, who achieved a remarkable total of fifteen broken nibs in one day. A record all the more astonishing as no actual play took place on the day concerned

Left: *An exciting moment in the scorebox. Moments as exciting as this are rare in the first-class game*

Right: *An exciting incident in the scorebox again. Excitement as great as this might happen less than once a season for the average scorer*

reliably measured at three-and-a-half inches square at the height of his fame. A four-foot square rubber, built specifically to beat the record by Oxford students in their rag week of 1956, broke up on the first erasure and was never officially employed in a match (the rules state that the rubber must be employed for a period of at least six consecutive hours). The practice of taking large rubbers into the score box is banned in Australia where in recent years three spectators have been bounced to death by rubbers falling out of the window above and landing on their heads.

NASTIEST INK BLOT EVER MADE BY A SCORER

The record for the ugliest ink blot made by a scorer goes to Daniel A. Arthbottle, the Lancashire scorer for many years, who in a hotly contested match in 1932 made an ink blot so ugly that he was grievously upset by the sight of it for many years and refused to be drawn on the topic when asked about it in conversation. The ink blot

was later framed and kept in the club trophy cabinet, where it became something of a talking point.

The Surrey scorer for the season 1912, D.H. Evans, made an ink blot that caused the match to be abandoned, on account of such profound ugliness that many believed it to be the work of the devil.

Nowadays, examples of ugly stains in score-books are far more rare, with the use of ball-point and felt-tip pens. There is no record of a record for the most ugly stain made by a felt-tip pen, and it would be pretty boring even if there was.

THE MOST SHORT-SIGHTED FIRST-CLASS SCORER

The most short-sighted first-class scorer must certainly be the Worcestershire scorer for the 1934 season, Barry Hardcastle, who succeeded in keeping the entire score for one match on the top of the wooden desk on which he was working. In another game, his glasses left at home, he managed to misread the entire match and ended up with the home team at 234,761 for 567 declared. His feats were quite legendary even among a score of equally capable misreaders who have in their time given a man out who died two years previously, and put down a score of 41,872 for a single ball.

THE SHINIEST PAIR OF TROUSERS EVER WORN BY A FIRST-CLASS SCORER

Shiny trouser seats, the trademark of the scorer, are a keenly fought-over item, many scorers having been known to spend hours at home slipping on and off leather armchairs to get the required level of shine. An iron is regularly used to brighten up the shine and, for that special occasion, shoe polish may be rubbed into the patch and buffed up to give a well-worn appearance. Probably the best example of shiny pants goes to the Nottinghamshire scorer F.H.T.P. Limpley, who wore the same set of trousers for over forty years, achieving a patch the shininess of which would be hard to match.

THE OLDEST EVER SUPPORTER

The oldest ever supporter was Bradfield J. Archer who supported Middlesex from the age of sixteen, and was aged 137 at the last game he attended in 1934. A post mortem revealed he had been dead for over thirty years and had been sitting there undisturbed since before the First World War. His record none the less stands and is unlikely to be beaten. The New Zealand Test Cricket Board recently reported a spectator of 141 still attending matches fifty-six years after his death but this claim was subsequently changed when he was found to be a player instead.

THE SPECTATOR WITH THE BIGGEST BOTTOM

The biggest bottom found on a spectator was on the rear end of Lord Elwyn Remarkably-Fetching whose rump, at its greatest extent, was measured at an astonishing 245 inches and required a full six seats in the pavilion at Tonbridge, where he was a regular supporter. So great was his girth that in one memorable match when the sightscreen sank into the turf and could not be moved, Elwyn was persuaded to take his bottom to the appropriate end of the ground and allow a white sheet to be draped over it.

THE MOST METICULOUS GROUNDSMAN

The record for the most meticulous and studious groundsman goes to Arnold Bucketthorpe, keeper of the Oval, Port Elizabeth, South Africa, who for more than thirty years insisted players remove their boots when entering the pavilion, whereupon he would carefully remove all dirt and grass from around the studs and aim to replace it in its original position on the pitch. Not only this but he refused to allow a match to continue when a wicket had been struck, and would immediately rush to the middle with microscope and tin of varnish and painstakingly repaint any blemish that might have been left as a result of the ball striking the stump. In England, the title of most meticulous groundsman must surely go to the legendary Aspinall P. Cravenhouse who succeeded in stopping a Test Match just so that a divot in the outfield could receive 'medical' treatment. The incident, coming as it did near the exciting climax on the final day, completely destroyed what had promised to be a close-fought series, especially when Cravenhouse insisted the area around the divot, including a portion of the wicket itself, be roped off to avoid any possible risk of further damage. Shortly after the incident Cravenhouse was retired from the game and spent his last remaining years in an Old Groundsman's Home in Buxton.

THE YOUNGEST GROUNDSMAN

The youngest groundsman in first-class cricket was the Kent man Daniel Spoade, who on his appointment in 1922 was just sixty-eight years old. Spoade, who at the time was a full twenty years younger than his nearest contemporary, was a controversial figure who went a long way to introducing some of the sweeping changes we now see in present day pitch-keeping. In 1936 his introduction of the long shovel, the short rake, the wide trowel and the six-inch 'dibber' shocked a game not ready for such controversy and he was forced to resign.

THE MOST OUTRAGEOUS REMARK BY A YORKSHIREMAN

The most outrageous remark ever spoken by a Yorkshireman came from the anonymous committee member who congratulated an opposing batsman after he had made an undefeated double century against the county. The member was never forgiven for the act and was forced to resign his seat as a result.

THE DEEPEST HOLE DUG BY A BATSMAN

The deepest hole dug by a batsman playing himself in was by the Indian opener Ravi Singh-Song, who in the course of a two-hour spell dug a two-foot crater in the wicket as he sought to establish control over the bowling. Eventually he fell into the hole he had dug and was clean bowled. An unauthenticated story, concerning a batsman in the officers' team involved in a match inside a Prisoner of War camp during the last War, tells how the officer dug himself in to such an extent that he completely disappeared from view and managed to dig a sixty-yard tunnel towards the camp fence that was only discovered by the Germans at the last possible moment. For the attempt the officer was placed in solitary confinement and had his Spear and Jackson cricket bat confiscated.

THE LEAST SENSIBLE APPEAL FOR A DISMISSAL

This must surely have occurred in the match between Blackrod and Newcombe in the North Yorkshire League when a batsman actually appealed for a dismissal against himself. It later transpired that the player was in the pay of the opposition and the ploy was a cunning attempt to lose the match for his own team without detection. The only rival to this claim as the least sensible appeal must go to the Chorleywood and Latimer captain who, in a 1938 match, claimed a wicket on the grounds that the batsman was too ugly to face his team's bowling. In the event the player

agreed to wear a box over his head to avoid upsetting the opposition and went on to hit a memorable fifty-two not out.

THE MOST EROGENOUS PART OF A CRICKETER'S BODY

The most erogenous part of a county cricketer's body is the small area of skin on the inside of his elbow. By nature, county cricketers suffer from an acute lack of erogenous zones, usually going for an entire career in the field without ever once feeling the slightest bit sexy.

The most erogenous parts of a cricketer's body (arrowed)

THE SHORTEST MATCH EVER PLAYED

The shortest match ever played was an amateur club game between Strawberry Vixen and The Leaf and Feather in the Taunton League. The match took place on 11 September 1960 in a driving gale. It became clear that neither team was eager to play and rather than rearrange the game for the following Saturday, when the football season started and the pitch would be needed, it was agreed to settle the match by, first, the home team declaring without playing a ball and then the opponent's team doing likewise. By this means the match was played in an extraordinary thirteen seconds. The home team won with a faster declaring rate. This is the only occasion of a match having been settled without a ball being bowled.

THE MOST EXCITING KIT EVER WORN BY A BATSMAN

Examples of unusual or fanciful clothing worn by cricketers abound. The most regular venue at which to appreciate such styles is the annual theatrical fancy dress cricket match played for the Green Room Trophy. In an exciting finish last season the Pantomime Goose and the Pantomime Cow required one run to win. In the result, the cow broke up mid-wicket and the match was tied. The most memorable example of unusual kit worn in a conventional match was in the Derbyshire v. Northamptonshire match of 1953 when the Derbyshire number 8 arrived late from a private function and had to go out to the wicket dressed as Tinkerbell the Magic Fairy. Unfortunately on his first scoring stroke he tripped over his wand and was run out.

THE GREATEST NUMBER OF CENTURIES OFF ONE BALL

Several cricketers have scored a century off one ball, most occurring before the present fixed boundary was introduced and a four or six awarded for balls passing over it. During this period one batsman, Cardigan Cosleton, had many a century off a single delivery, his favourite ploy being to drive the ball into the duck pond alongside his local ground where fielders would spend hours searching the muddy waters for it. Only one man has achieved the feat of one hundred runs off one ball under the more restricting rules of today, the ball landing in a patch of clover, whereupon a grazing sheep that had strayed on to the field took it in its mouth and swallowed it whole. Eventually, after Cosleton had run 138 runs, the fielders, who were waiting for the sheep to pass the ball, picked up the animal and carried it to the wicket, tossing it against the stumps in a bid to run the batsman out. After a heated argument the dismissal was rejected and a new ball was found in the umpire's coat.

THE GREATEST NUMBER OF TIMES A BATSMAN HAS BEEN GIVEN OUT BY AN UMPIRE IN ONE INNINGS

This record must certainly go to Marius Blankfurt, a keen cricketer and master of disguise. In a match with the village side of Penbury-cum-Martin, he won the toss and elected to bat. It was not till the close of the innings, when it was his turn to field, that his trick was rumbled and the umpire realised that Blankfurt had returned from the pavilion ten times, on each occasion in different disguise, and had therefore batted in all eleven positions. This is the only recorded example of a batsman being given out ten times in the same game by the same umpire. Blankfurt was not able to repeat his feat in the field and the village team ran out easy winners.

CHAPTER TWENTY-ONE

CRICKET TODAY

CRICKET today is enjoying an unexpected revival. Let us look at the reasons for this and also at some of the plans to make it even more popular.

ONE-DAY CRICKET

Undoubtedly one of the main reasons for this upsurge in interest is the one-day game. To the purist a match played in what amounts to an afternoon is still an insult – the equivalent of an eighteen-minute match for the footballer or a twenty-five-metre medley relay for the swimmer. One-day cricket has brought in huge crowds. It appeals to a completely new type of cricket supporter – usually called a football supporter.

Below: *The bowling aim in one-day cricket*

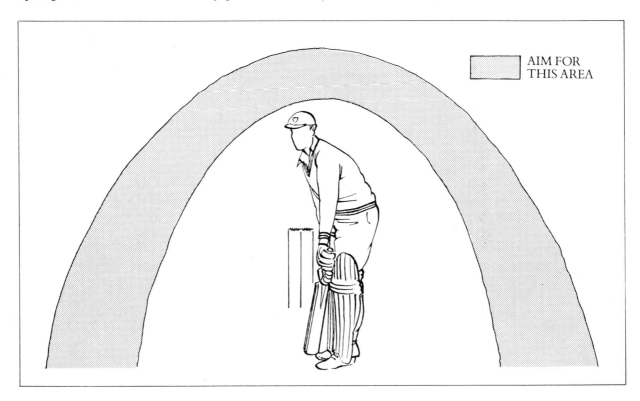

AIM FOR
THIS AREA

ONE-DAY FIELDING

The principal difference for the fielder between one-day cricket and conventional cricket is the need to *stay alert*. The five-day match usually allows players in the field to operate a rota system whereby at any time only half the fielders remain awake and the rest are asleep on their feet, only to be woken and called into action if alerted by a colleague. By contrast the one-day fielder may well have to field a number of balls in quick succession, some of which may require *agility and speed*. The sort of fellow adept at this type of work is more likely to be found between the posts on a first division football ground, few cricketers being keen to splay themselves in a diving sprawl simply to stop a batsman making one extra run. Unless they are Derek Randall.

One-day cricket is often called 'limited over' cricket, the game being prescribed by a limited number of overs. The alternative type of limited over game is limited to the period between afternoon closing and the time they open up again in the evening and is usually called 'village cricket'.

SPONSORSHIP

Associated with the one-day game and now very much a part of the game at all levels. The names of sponsors involved with the game are now extremely well known, although commercial intervention in the rules and regulations of cricket has been kept in check. Players do *not* stroll out on to the wicket with a cigarette in one hand, a pint of lager in the other, and a life insurance policy stuck in the pocket. However, in a series of confidentially leaked documents, evidence has emerged to suggest players have been encouraged to patronise sponsors' products:

PLAYER   Left arm round the wicket, umpire.
UMPIRE   Excuse me – are you feeling all right?
PLAYER   What? Yes, of course.
UMPIRE   I just thought you looked a bit . . . peaky.
PLAYER   Never felt fitter.

UMPIRE   You don't look very well . . . you're sure you're not about to faint?
PLAYER   Look, I feel fine! Can I start my over now, please?
UMPIRE   I mean you don't look all that bad, but that's often the worst possible sign.
PLAYER   Look, I feel fine, now can we please get on with the game!
UMPIRE   By the way, have you always been unsteady on your feet like that?
PLAYER   Oh for heaven's sake . . .
UMPIRE   I don't suppose, heaven forbid, anything should happen to you, and I'm not suggesting for a second it will but . . . well, would you read this from me . . . as a friend . . .
PLAYER   What is it?
UMPIRE   Just sign here . . .
PLAYER   Wait a minute, this is a Life Assurance proposal form made out in my name and with my details.
UMPIRE   Sorry, can't stop – left arm round the wicket did you say, speak to you at the end of the over!

Early trials of a new type of cricket devised to promote a certain brand of beer

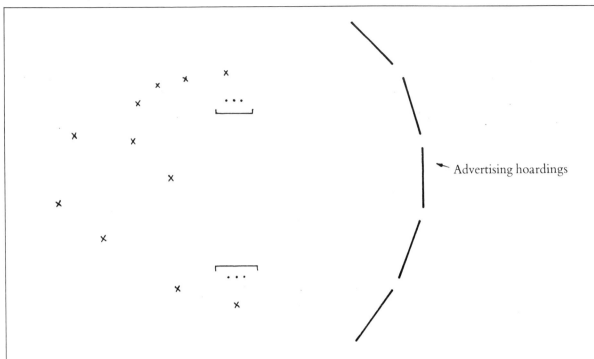

→ Advertising hoardings

Above: *Optimum field positions for a fielding team wishing to maximise coverage of sponsors' hoardings*

Below: *Optimum advertising positions. Many Counties are actively considering advertising on the players' dress. These three examples show the optimum 'site' for any potential advertisement in particular situations*

WICKET-KEEPER'S BUM

ENGLAND FAST BOWLER

WEST INDIAN FAST BOWLER

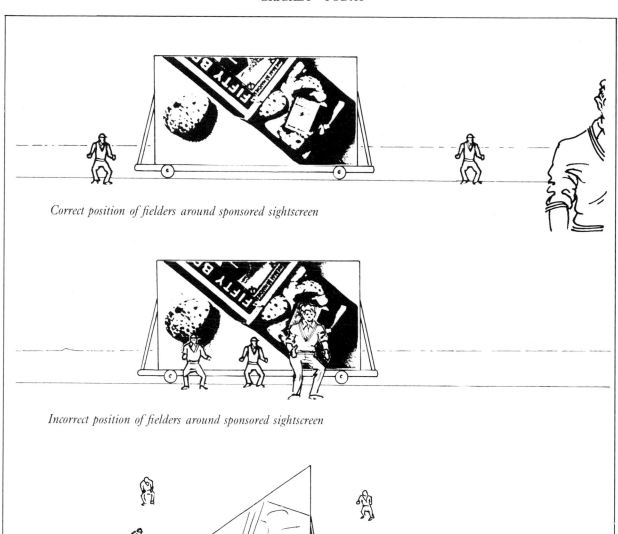

Correct position of fielders around sponsored sightscreen

Incorrect position of fielders around sponsored sightscreen

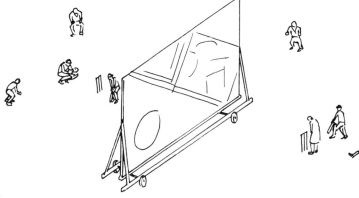

Incorrect position of sponsored sightscreen around field

ADVERTISING
CAMPAIGNS
THAT FAILED

Right: *Playtex lifts, holds, separates*

Below: *Everest Double Glazing*

Andrex

Correct positioning of slip fielders for promotion campaign

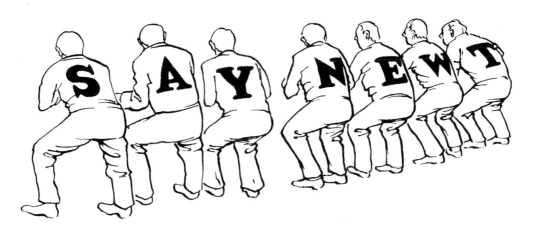

Incorrect positioning of same fielders for promotion in same campaign

TWENTY-FOUR HOUR CRICKET

The use of white balls, yellow kit and floodlights has been developed in Australia with reasonable support. Moreover, the idea of making cricket available at a time when spectators wish to see it, and not during the day when they are at work, has to be considered over here. In line with this, a number of additional suggestions are now being made.

Breakfast Cricket Play starts at 6.30 a.m. and continues till 9.30 a.m. Players wear light casual kit and must be prepared to join in a light chat with guest interviewers between overs. Regular news and weather intervals.

Lunchtime Cricket   Played between 12 noon and 2.00 p.m. (Not to be confused with Brunch Cricket which is played between Breakfast and Lunchtime, and also Elevenses Cricket which is played for fifteen minutes between eleven and quarter past.)

Tea-time Cricket   Played between 3.00 p.m. and 3.30 p.m. The first team bats for five minutes, followed by a twenty-minute tea interval, followed by the second team batting for five minutes.

Overnight Cricket   Played for the benefit of insomniacs, nightshift workers and also for *live broadcast* during the middle of the day to countries on the other side of the world. Thus English supporters wishing to see their team play live have the option either of watching a day-time match live in their own country, or a night-time match live on the opposite side of the world.

TEN-DAY CRICKET

The opposite of the one-day game. Players aim to stay at the wicket long enough to prevent the game ever developing into a contest. Scoring shots are discouraged (as featured in the film *They Shoot Cricket Supporters Don't They?*). A strong lobby from Yorkshire supports this type of cricket.

TELEVISION

Players should be aware of the need to offer entertainment to the television audience. Those taking part should note that all shots are made only with the prior consent of the television producer who has sole discretion to select sides and players he feels provide maximum entertainment irrespective of playing ability. Controversial incidents are warmly received by television, and players wishing to embark upon a career in the media upon retirement are advised to develop outlandish behaviour that will capture the camera's attention. Rudeness, belligerence, or sheer cussedness that might not normally be tolerated will be handsomely rewarded in the televised match. Try to develop a peculiar or unusual personal habit for television exposure. Exotic hair is useful (Botham) and weight problems regularly attract attention (Botham). Other *sub judice* practices have also proved remunerative (Botham).

MA

1 Death
oquist
himsel

2 Abdul
by runn

3 Swiss C

4 Swiss C

5 Rubber
1894.

6 England
Third Te

7 1926 – M
seven feet
squashed

8 Nympho
cricket vid

9 Automatic,
introduced
men seriou
removed by

10 Monty Gor
tragically di
leg so hard

11 Andrew Ma
Test umpire

12 'Denis Comp
1950.

13 'Denis Compt
1950.

14 'Denis Compto
go on sale 195

15 'Geoffrey Boyc
WAIT ... SO
shirts go on sal

16 Medal struck to
so gallantly in
Matches.

17 Harrow School s
catches to the ma
game.

18 New Zealand Cric
sheep on the origi

206

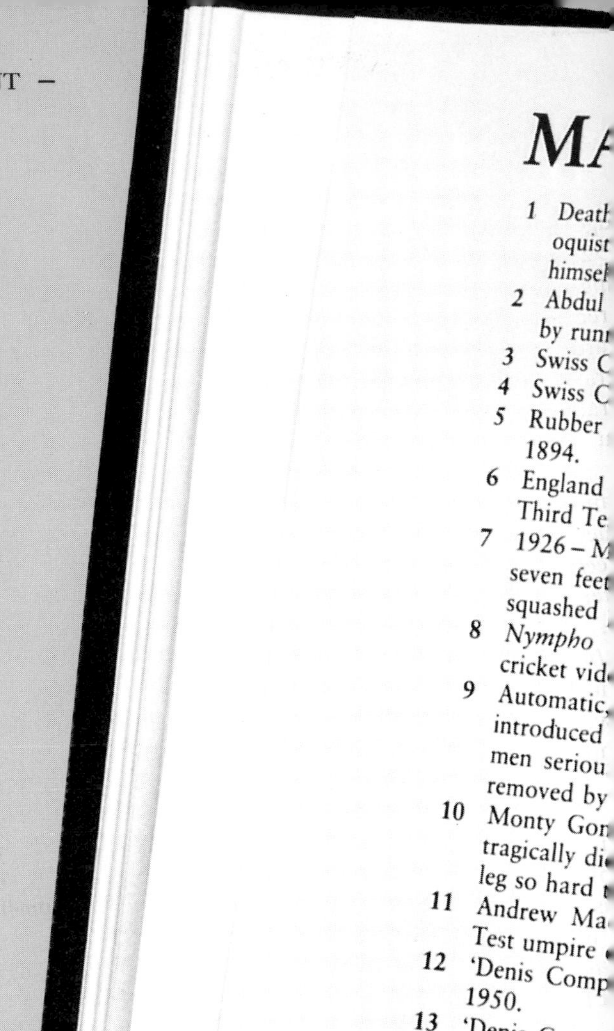

dge Elliot, the world's first ventril-
921, well known for appealing to
ing his own voice.

red minus sixteen runs in one over
ards, 1952.

ration formed 1934.

ration dissolved 1933.

t banned from first-class game

and, English team eaten alive in
ley 1873).

eek – world's largest cricket ball.
ference. Two batsmen seriously

In Love – first pornographic
in London shops 1978.

vered, pad-fastening machine
mptonshire dressing-room; two
Third has to have his smile

ndian very very fast bowler.
bing a cricket ball against his
sers ignite.

becomes the youngest-ever
fourth birthday.

ELAX' T-shirts go on sale

WZAT' T-shirts go on sale

– A QUICK ONE' T-shirts

...NO...YES...NO,
D I SAY SORRY!?' T-

ate those who have died
ress Tents during Test

wn for refusing to give
nnual Masters v. Boys

on formed 1882 (eight
e).

19 Mounted cricket attempted 1907.

20 Wormwood Scrubs Inter-wing Cricket Cup ends in confusion as eighteen players attempt to go over the wall to fetch a ball that hasn't even been delivered.

21 1961 . . . Barston Hickson, inventor of the cardboard jock-strap, dies a very broken man indeed.

22 1957 . . . Deighton Asprey, the noted geographer, publishes a paper in which he reveals that if the present trends of continental drift continue, then the West Indies will become part of the British Isles in fifty billion years' time and West Indian players will become eligible for English selection (not Yorkshire).

23 1861 – Anniversary of the first English foreign tour to Wales. Wales won.

24 1952 – Three English cricketers defect to Russia. Last heard playing in the Siberia and District Sunday League.

25 Birthday of Arnold Bastroff – the man who invented the cricket pavilion door that wouldn't shut properly.

26 Cricket Supporters' Wives Remembrance Day.

27 1964 – Record number of jumpers worn by a cricket umpire set – twenty-seven, plus two coats.

28 Ian Chappell School of Cricket Etiquette opens in Australia, 1981. Three men arrested for brawling on enrolment day.

29 Ian Chappell School of Cricket Etiquette names Bob Hawke its Life President.

30 'No Balls' day in Commonwealth countries.

31 Ceylon Cricket Federation decides to allow fifteen minute 'cricket match' in between morning and afternoon tea intervals.

32 Long Stumps Day, Jamaica.

33 Annual Combined Services *v.* Lady Bothferry Girls High School.

34 Opening Day of 'Removals', Old Ground, York.

35 Birthday of Greg Dipple, Australian slow left-arm drinker.

36 Old Flannels Day, Harrogate.

37 Sombre-Latimer died, 1931, inventor of the Ritchie Benaud.

38 Ceremony of 'Long Leg' held on Long Thicktickle Edge.

39 1896 – W.G. Gross scores one thousand runs before the end of May.